MONSTERS
OF ILLINOIS

Mysterious Creatures in the Prairie State

Troy Taylor

STACKPOLE
BOOKS

Published by
STACKPOLE BOOKS
5067 Ritter Road
Mechanicsburg, PA 17055
www.stackpolebooks.com

Printed in the United States of America

10 9 8 7 6 5 4 3 2 1

FIRST EDITION

Cover art by Mark Radle
Cover design by Tessa J. Sweigert

Library of Congress Cataloging-in-Publication Data

Taylor, Troy.
  Monsters of Illinois : mysterious creatures in the Prairie State / Troy Taylor. — 1st ed.
      p. cm.
  Includes bibliographical references (p.   ).
  ISBN-13: 978-0-8117-3640-4 (pbk.)
  ISBN-10: 0-8117-3640-7 (pbk.)
  1. Monsters—Illinois. I. Title.
  QL89.T355 2011
  001.944—dc22

                                    2011008647

CONTENTS

INTRODUCTION

I have had a lifelong fascination with the mysterious and the unexplained. I've also had an obsessive interest in the history and mystery of my home state of Illinois. Those interests combined during my childhood as I sought out stories of Illinois ghosts, unsolved crimes, and general weirdness. I was intrigued by just about any mysterious happenings but was particularly thrilled when I heard that someone spotted a big hairy monster somewhere in the state.

I grew up on a farm in rural Illinois and spent countless hours roaming the state's fields and forests, once having a strange encounter of my own that will turn up later in this book. My brother and I often disappeared for hours—and sometimes days—at a time, always wondering if we might stumble across ancient burial mounds or mysterious structures in the hills and forests. One summer we spent weeks excavating a mound in the woods in search of ancient artifacts, only to find that the rise was nothing more than an oddly shaped hill. We were disappointed but undeterred.

As I got older, my explorations often found me in some of the state's strangest places, from small towns in southern Illinois where unusual monsters had been reported to the Bigfoot-infested woods of the Illinois River Valley. I was able to relive some of those weird travels in writing this book. In the pages that follow, we'll explore the mysteries that still linger in Illinois—a place stranger than many of us can imagine.

Did you know there are stories of a flying monster that plagued Illinois even before the first settlers arrived?

Did you know that Illinois boasts more Bigfoot sightings than any other state east of the Mississippi River?

Did you know that during the 1970s, Illinois was "under attack" by huge flying creatures that were never explained?

This book will delve into each of these stories, along with many others, and will hopefully introduce you to things about the state that you never knew before. Most important, though, I hope that this book will encourage you to get out and explore some of the Illinois places where monsters dwell. You will be following in my footsteps, just as I followed in those of others, and while it's been a long, strange trip, it's been a good one. Happy hunting!

Bigfoot in Illinois

I have always had a love for the "wild" regions of Illinois. Growing up, I spent every possible minute outdoors; my fascination with the forests, lakes, and rivers of the state went hand in hand with my interest in the unusual. For this reason, I always listened closely to the frequent reports of sightings of wild and mysterious creatures in the dark woods and remote regions of Illinois.

There is no greater mystery in the annals of the unexplained in America than Sasquatch, the creature more commonly known as Bigfoot. Reports of giant man- and apelike monsters have been documented all over the country. There are many tales of giant hairy figures in every state in America, including Illinois, which is said to have more Bigfoot sightings than any other state east of the Mississippi River.

According to scores of eyewitnesses, Sasquatch average around seven feet in height, sometimes taller and sometimes a little shorter. They are usually seen wandering alone, and dark, auburn-colored hair covers most of their bodies, although reports of brown, black, and even white and silver Bigfoot do occasionally pop up. Their limbs are usually powerful but are described as being proportioned more like those of people than those of apes. However, their broad shoulders, short necks, flat faces and noses, sloped foreheads, ridged brows, and

3

cone-shaped heads make them appear more animal-like. They reportedly eat both meat and plants, are largely nocturnal, and are less active during cold weather. The footprints left behind by the monsters range in length from about twelve to twenty-two inches, with around eighteen inches being the most common. They are normally reported to be somewhere around seven inches in width.

The stories of Sasquatch and other hairy, man-like creatures have been part of American history since the days of the Native Americans. Even the term "Sasquatch" was taken from Native American mythology. The folkloric Sasquatch (the word is the Anglicized version of the Coast Salish Indian term from Canada) was introduced to the world in the writings of J. W. Burns, a schoolteacher at the Chehalis Indian Reservation near Harrison Hot Springs, British Columbia. Burns's Sasquatch was a legendary figure that he learned of through native informants. He was really more man than monster, an intelligent "giant Indian" who was endowed with supernatural powers. Somehow, the name managed to stick for the huge beings that came to be called Bigfoot.

Stories of Bigfoot began filtering out of the American West in the early 1900s, occasionally appearing in newspaper accounts and books. Bigfoot did not enter the American mainstream until 1958, when a series of footprints was found near a construction site in California. Over the course of the next thirty years or so, interest in the elusive creatures reached a fever pitch.

By the 1960s, Bigfoot had become firmly entrenched in the imaginations of Americans. Although scientists were skeptical that such creatures could exist, a number of investigators had begun seeking out witnesses and venturing into the forest, hoping to catch a glimpse of one of the monsters. Books began to appear and articles generated even more interest among the readers of magazines like *True* and *Saga*.

Among the amateur investigators who went looking for Bigfoot was Roger Patterson, a onetime rodeo rider and hopeful documentary filmmaker. In 1967, Patterson was barely scraping by as an inventor and promoter but his interest was piqued by a *True* magazine article about Bigfoot. From then on, he devoted as much of his spare time as he could afford roaming the woods of the Pacific Northwest in search of the creature. Patterson always carried with him a motion-picture camera on his expeditions, hoping that he might be able to catch one of the monsters on film.

Around 1:15 in the afternoon on October 20, 1967, Patterson and a friend, Bob Gimlin, were riding north along a dry stretch of Bluff Creek in the Six Rivers National Forest of northern California. At one point, a large pile of logs in the middle of the streambed blocked their path and they had to maneuver their horses around to the east. As they rode along the logs, they veered left and resumed their original course, only to see something that still has investigators and researchers puzzled today.

What was believed to be a female Bigfoot stood up from the water where she had been squatting and hurried away from the approaching men and horses, moving briskly and swinging her arms as she walked toward the forest. At the same time this occurred, the horses began to panic. Patterson quickly reached for the 16mm camera in his saddlebag and began to follow the creature, filming as he went. Unfortunately, only twenty-eight feet of film remained in the camera, but Patterson managed to use it to record the Bigfoot's escape from three different filming positions.

After he returned home, Patterson enlisted the help of researcher John Green to get some sort of scientific confirmation of the evidence that he had captured. The first investigator sent to the scene of the sighting was a man named Bob Titmus, who found tracks that matched the creature's stride as depicted in the film. He made ten casts of them and discovered that the footprints led up a small hill where the creature had paused to look back on the men below. Patterson and Gimlin had elected to recover their horses rather than pursue the Bigfoot and risk being stranded in the wilderness.

After being ignored, then berated, by the established scientific community, Patterson took his evidence to the public in 1968. After padding his film footage with a documentary-style look at other evidence gathered in the search for Bigfoot, he went on a tour of the American West, renting small theaters and auditoriums for one-night shows and lectures. Since that time, the footage has gone on to become one of the most famous, and most controversial, pieces of Bigfoot evidence ever found.

Patterson's life was cut short in 1972 when he died, nearly broke, from Hodgkin's disease, but he swore to the end that the sighting and the film were authentic. Bob Gimlin also maintained that the events really took place and that his friend's film was the genuine article. Gimlin did not start out as a believer in the creature, either. He was interested but unconvinced and only came along on his buddy's expeditions out of friendship, rather than a belief that they would actually find anything. "He'd talk about it around the campfire," Gimlin said in an interview. "I didn't care, but after a time you'd find yourself looking for the doggone thing too."

The legacy of Patterson's film lives on. Unfortunately, it has never settled the question of whether or not Bigfoot exists in the forests of America. Bigfoot researchers remain divided about whether or not the creature in the film is genuine. They have argued about the speed of the film, the gait of the creature, the distance of its stride, and more. Most biologists and zoologists who have studied it remain noncommittal. Film experts and hoax investigators can find nothing to say that it's not real, only that it's hard to believe. To this day, it's never successfully been debunked, creating a mystery much like the mystery of Bigfoot itself.

Tales of Bigfoot have long been a part of Illinois history and lend an air of mystery to the state that is unrivaled by any other region of the Midwest. For more than a century, reports have filtered out of rural and southern Illinois about strange beasts that resemble a cross between man and ape. Most witnesses talk of the beasts' odd appearance and the horrible odor that seems to accompany them. The stories of these creatures have been passed along from generation to generation and have long been chronicled by both professional and amateur researchers.

The earliest documented Illinois sighting came in September 1883 and concerned a "wild man" that was seen in the woods near Centreville. This was a common term at the time, when a moniker like "Bigfoot" had not yet been coined and no reader was familiar with a creature of that sort. Even the idea of an "ape" was completely foreign, as the great apes of Africa were not discovered until late in the century. For this reason, a search through old periodicals will not reveal historical Bigfoot accounts; what did sometimes appear in newspapers of the 1800s were stories of "wild men" and beast-like creatures that were encountered, sometimes captured, and occasionally killed. These reports likely thrilled readers of the day and may offer the modern researcher the first true reports of Bigfoot in America.

The "wild man" reported in Centreville was described as a "naked roaming madman" who had been "roaming around the country" for several days, causing "intense excitement and consternation" for the rural folks who lived in and around the small community. The man was described as having a long dark beard and being covered with matted hair. He had a tall "athletic form" and a fierce look in his eyes that made him "exceedingly unpleasant to meet in a lonely spot." The creature was seen by the wife of Dr. John Saltenberger, who was returning home shortly after nightfall when she saw it creeping out of the orchard on her property. The wild man made a quick rush toward her horse and buggy but Mrs. Saltenberger frantically turned her whip on him and then snapped the reins of the horse to increase her speed. The horse picked up the pace but the creature stayed close behind and then suddenly leapt onto the back of the carriage. He only remained there for a few moments before jumping down and running into the woods. Needless to say, Mrs. Saltenberger was terrified by the encounter and the following day, her husband placed a telephone call to Belleville and asked the sheriff to come and capture the creature. The sheriff was joined in his hunt by several young men from the area. Despite a thorough search of the woods around Centreville, the monster never turned up.

The next report came from 1912. A woman named Beulah Schroat reported that she and her brothers often encountered hairy creatures in the woods near their home outside of Effingham. According to her description, the beasts stood on their hind legs and were about as tall as normal people, with large eyes and copious amounts of hair. The creatures seemed very shy and harmless and always ran away whenever they were approached. They were usually seen near a small creek on the farm, where they waded and splashed about. Ms. Schroat said that her brothers would often run to the house after an encounter but their parents dismissed the stories as practical jokes until they found an article about similar monsters in a Chicago newspaper.

The next documented account was a brief report about a manlike beast, covered in brown hair, which was spotted near Alton in 1925. There are unfortunately no other details to accompany this account.

Another report comes not long after the Alton sighting. In this brief snippet, we find that a "huge gorilla" was seen in the woods near Elizabeth in July 1929. Then, in 1941, the Reverend Lepton Harpole was hunting squirrels near Mount Vernon and encountered a large creature that "looked something like a baboon." He struck it with his rifle and fired a warning shot that sent it scurrying back into the underbrush. More sightings of the same creature occurred the next year and searches were conducted along the Gun Creek Bottoms in hopes of tracking the animal down. More than 1,500 men attempted to flush out the beast, which was said to have a "wildcat's scream," combing the bottoms with shotguns and rifles at the ready. After the attack on Reverend Harpole, the animal was also blamed for the death of a dog in the vicinity. No trace of it was ever found.

From the 1940s and into the 1960s, huge prints were discovered along the marshy areas of Indian Creek in southwestern Illinois. The creature leaving the tracks was dubbed the "Gooseville Bear," taking its name from an area of farmland and small businesses located about three miles east of Bethalto where Route 140 crosses Indian Creek. History has it that the informal name was bestowed on the community in the 1850s when farm geese would follow grain wagons in hopes of finding stray corn and wheat. Some identified the tracks as belonging to a bear but others insisted that they were manlike. Whatever the beast was, it was never seen, and after leaving its mark on the area for almost two decades, it disappeared.

In 1962, Steven Collins and Robert Earle spotted a grayish-colored creature standing in a riverbed east of Decatur, just off of East Williams Street Road. The monster was standing upright in the water, looking straight at them. At first, they thought they were seeing a bear, until they noticed its strange, humanlike features. The creature vanished into the woods and the witnesses told the local newspaper that it was "like no other animal we had ever seen before."

In May 1963, eighty years after the rash of "wild man" sightings in Centreville, another strange creature reared its ugly head in the town just across the Mississippi from St. Louis. The initial reports of it actually came from St. Louis, when several children reported a "half man, half woman with a half bald head and a half head of hair." It was said to have been seen lurking around the Ninth Street housing project and often disappeared into an old tunnel around Twelfth Street. The sightings were taken quite seriously by Patrolman Bill Conreux of the St. Louis Police Department. He noted that "Those kids were sincere. They saw something." He added that the creature supposedly "scuffled with a man near the Patrick Henry School."

The first sightings were on May 9. By May 18, it had moved east across the river to Centreville, which is located near East St. Louis and Cahokia. One man, James McKinney, described it as being "half man and half horse." It made an appearance just in front of his house and he summoned the police, who never managed to catch up with this mysterious figure. According to reports, the authorities received more than fifty calls in a single night about this creature. The sightings eventually dropped off and by May 23, the monster was apparently gone. Others claim that sightings of the creature continued around Centreville until the 1980s but were never publicized.

In September 1965, four young people were parked in a car near an undeveloped area outside of Decatur called Montezuma Hills. The area would later become a housing development, but at that time, it was a secluded "lover's lane." The young couples were sitting in the car when a black, manlike shape approached the vehicle. The creature seemed massive and it frightened the teenagers badly. They drove off in a panic, but after dropping off their dates at home, the two young men returned to the area for another look. They once again saw the monster, and it walked up to their car as though it was curious. The boys were too scared to get out, but even with the windows rolled up, they could smell the monster's terrible stench. They quickly summoned the police to the site and with several officers as support, they made a thorough but fruitless search of the woods. The police officers on the scene said they had no idea what the young people had witnessed, but they were obviously very frightened by whatever it had been.

Another manlike creature was encountered near Chittyville in August 1968. Two young people, Tim Bullock and Barbara Smith, were driving north of town on August 11 when they spotted a ten-foot-tall monster that was covered with black hair and had a round face. It threw dirt at their car and they left to summon the police. When the authorities arrived, they found a large depression in the grass that was apparently a nest. Local residents claimed that their dogs had been "carrying on" for the two weeks before the sighting.

Another frightening encounter occurred about one month later, in September 1968, a few miles outside of Carpentersville in Cook County. Two young men were driving along some back roads, searching for a party they had been invited to, and got lost somewhere east of what is now Barrington Hills. They started to turn around to drive back towards Carpentersville. That's when they saw something at the edge of the road. A creature, which one of the men stated was "about as tall as our Ford van," started out across the roadway, about fifteen to twenty feet in front of their vehicle. The creature had a long stride, stood upright, and was covered with dark brown (almost black) hair that was matted and longer in some spots. It swung its arms as it walked, in a manner that suggested the arms were too long for its torso, and as it crossed the road, it turned and looked at the two men. Its face was also covered with hair but there was little around the eyes, nose, and mouth. The witnesses stated that its face was flat, more like a person's than an ape's. As the driver was backing up and quickly turning the vehicle around, the passenger looked to his right as they pulled away. What he saw gave him quite a fright—the creature had changed directions, as if it planned to chase their van. They were terrified because "it looked so powerful that it could have torn the doors off the van with no trouble whatsoever." They immediately left the area and did not return for another look.

A violent encounter with some sort of hairy monster occurred about one month later, in October 1968, just outside of Lewiston in Fulton County. One Friday evening, around 9:30 P.M., three high school boys were riding in a truck, following a friend in his own car near the Dutch Henry crossing. The boys in the truck were forced to stop abruptly when they saw their friend's car was now parked crosswise in the road in front of them. In their headlights, they could see their friend lying on the road, seemingly unconscious. The young men got out of the truck and were walking toward their fallen friend when someone, or something, came out of the darkness and knocked them to the ground. Each time they tried to get up, they were knocked back down again. The boys later reported that whatever the assailant was, it did not hit them with its fists but instead backhanded them with terrific force. At one point, the boys did manage to wrestle the creature to the ground but it knocked them aside with ease. During the struggle, the first boy, who had been on the ground, ran for the truck and locked the doors. He said that he got a fairly good look at the creature and that it was not too tall but it was very powerfully built and seemed to be very hairy. Too terrified to get out of the truck, the boy remained there until the monster finally ran off into the woods. The boys were not badly harmed but they were shaken up and the incident was reported to the local police. No trace of the creature was ever found.

One of the strangest Illinois incidents took place near Farmer City in July 1970. Early that spring, three sheep had been killed near town but local officials dismissed it as the work of wild dogs, which had been known to roam the area. The slaughtered animals would later be connected to incidents near Salt Creek, a ten-acre section of woods outside of town that was popular with teenagers.

Three young men decided to camp out there one night and, later that evening, they reported hearing something approaching their campsite through the tall grass. They turned a light in the direction of the sounds and saw a huge, black shape crouching near the tent. The shape had a pair of gleaming, yellow eyes, which was a color that would be repeated in every account to follow. The terrified screams of the teenagers frightened the creature and it vanished into the woods.

Stories about the "Farmer City Monster" quickly spread. Dozens of people reported seeing the creature over the next several days and all of the sightings took place near the wooded area along Salt Creek. Robert Hayslip, a Farmer City police officer who investigated the scene, reported his own encounter. In the early-morning hours of July 15, he saw the broad back of the creature moving among the trees. The creature turned in his direction and Hayslip also noted its yellow eyes. Although initially skeptical of the creature's existence, the Farmer City police chief decided to close off the woods to visitors.

The creature soon moved on. On July 24, a couple driving near Weldon Springs State Park, outside of Clinton, saw what looked like a huge bear in the river. Later, a policeman and a conservation officer found tracks along the water's edge that definitely did not belong to a bear. They were reportedly very large and humanlike.

A few days later, farther north, a woman caught the reflection of yellow eyes in her car headlights as she was traveling outside of Bloomington. She thought the eyes might belong to a dog that had been injured by a passing car, so she stopped and walked back along the edge of the road. Suddenly, a large creature jumped out of the ditch and ran away on two legs. She was unsure about what she had seen, but whatever it was, it seemed apelike. Later that same week, another witness reported an identical creature near Heyworth.

On August 11, three young men reported seeing a large, dark-haired creature near Waynesville, and five days later, construction workers saw the creature near the same location. It ran across the highway in front of their truck and disappeared into the forest. That was the last report of the so-called Farmer City Monster. One can't help but wonder if it continued its strange journey northwest across central Illinois. If it did, it was never reported again.

In 1971, twelve-year-old Doug Dunbar accompanied his father on overnight guard duty during the construction of the Rend Lake Dam, near Benton. Doug's father, a Franklin County deputy sheriff and state's attorney investigator, was locking the gates at 5:00 A.M. when they heard dogs barking in the distance and the sounds of someone running through the grass nearby. Mr. Dunbar told Doug to turn on the car headlights and that was when they saw "something" hunched over and standing in the middle of the road about fifty yards in front of the vehicle. After looking into the headlights for a few moments, it made a giant leap and disappeared into the ditch alongside the road. "I was absolutely terrified," Doug told me more than thirty years later. "Dad investigated with his flashlight to find nothing but barking dogs and a barbed wire fence. The smell was dreadful. To this day, I have no explanation for what we saw."

In May 1972, new reports came from the Pekin and Peoria areas. In late May, a young man named Randy Emmert, along with some friends, reported a large, hairy creature near Cole Hollow Road. This monster was between eight and ten feet tall and whitish in color. The witnesses stated that it made a loud, screeching sound and they suspected that it was living in a hole beneath an abandoned house. It also left very unusual tracks, having only three toes on each foot. Soon, others were reporting the same monster and it became known as "Cohomo," short for the "Cole Hollow Road Monster."

On May 25, local police logged more than two hundred calls about the monster, including one where the creature destroyed a fence. The police officers were naturally skeptical, but the calls kept coming in. By July 1972, there had been so many sightings that one hundred volunteers were organized to search for Cohomo. Eventually, Tazewell County sheriff's deputies sent the volunteers home after one of them, Carl R. Harris, accidentally shot himself in the leg with a .22-caliber pistol.

The sightings continued and they couldn't be written off to local hysteria either. One witness, from Eureka, knew nothing about the creature, yet happened to be in Fondulac Park in East Peoria for a birthday party. He reported seeing the creature and as well as a set of strange lights that seemed to descend vertically and land behind some trees. Were the two sightings connected? No one knows, but whatever the creature was, it was gone.

In July 1972, strangeness came to the town of Cairo, which is at the southernmost tip of the state. On Tuesday evening, July 25, a huge, white-colored monster was spotted by a local man named LeRoy Summers. He told police that he had seen the creature, which he claimed was at least ten feet tall, standing by a small brick building on the Ohio River levee between 28th and 17th Streets. Summers said that he was jogging on the levee when he saw the creature. He didn't stay around long enough to get a look at the monster's facial features, but he did note that it had a large head, as well as a solid white, hairy body with a tinge of red around its middle. When police officers returned to the scene, they could find no sign of the creature; as the patrolmen were returning to the station, another sighting was called in. This new search also proved to be fruitless and the monster was not heard from again.

Later that year, in September 1972, another weird encounter occurred near the small farming community of Kell in Marion County. The sighting was not reported for many years, largely thanks to the remote location, but the woman involved had vivid memories of the day.

One fall afternoon, a woman who resided near Kell spotted a very large, beige-colored creature at the edge of the woods near her home. The house was surrounded on three sides by cornfields and then a densely wooded area made up the fourth side of the yard. The only access to the house was by way of a gravel drive. At the time of the sighting, the corn had been harvested from the fields near the house, leaving a wide expanse of open area.

The witness was talking on the telephone with her mother when the family dogs, several beagles, began making a terrible racket. After quickly putting down the telephone receiver, she went and looked out from the screened porch. As she did, her eyes were drawn to the woods, where she saw the creature crouched down. Thinking that perhaps it was a bear, she picked up the telephone and described it to her mother. As she was doing so, the dogs began barking and howling and then ran towards the monster, stopping several feet away from it. They continued to bark but would not go any closer to it. Suddenly, the hairy monster stood upright and looked toward the house. It stumbled forward and the dogs turned and began to run away. Even though her mother insisted that she not go outside, the witness hurried to the screen door and called to the dogs. The beagles, never afraid of anything, were frantic and dashed to the open door.

The monster stood for a few more moments, looking toward the house, and then turned and shambled back into the trees.

As soon as it disappeared, the dogs immediately settled down and acted as though nothing out of the usual had happened. The witness, however, did not soon forget what she had seen.

The next monster event occurred in Decatur during the summer of 1973. Three men who were walking along the Sangamon River one afternoon saw a large, hairy man that looked like an ape. The sighting took place just south of the city, outside of Greenwood Cemetery, in a wooded area that many local residents know as Hell Hollow. This area was known for many years as a "hobo jungle," because homeless people would often hop freight trains that passed nearby. It was not uncommon to see unkempt, and perhaps even "hairy" men in ragged clothing in this vicinity. According to the witnesses however, this "hairy man" was different. Not only was he unclothed, but he also stood much taller than an average person and appeared to be very animallike. The monster was seen near the river for several moments but when it realized that it was being observed, it darted into the underbrush. The witnesses, understandably, declined to pursue it.

On June 6, 1973, police in Edwardsville received three reports of a large, humanlike creature with a terrible smell that was seen lurking in the woods east of town. The creature was broad-shouldered but short and reportedly made no sound when it walked. The witnesses claimed that the thing chased them and one man told the police that the creature had clawed at him and ripped his shirt. There were three total sightings, two on June 4 and one on June 8, and all took place in a wooded area near Mooney, Little Mooney, and Sugar Creeks.

Then, a few weeks later, the town of Murphysboro in southwestern Illinois became the scene of a series of monster sightings. The enigmatic creature appeared without warning and then disappeared just two weeks later, seemingly without a trace. In its wake, the monster left a number of confused and frightened witnesses, baffled law enforcement officials, and of course, an enduring legend.

Throughout the 1970s, many sketchy reports of Bigfoot sightings made news in Illinois, especially in the Shawnee National Forest and the American Bottoms region along the Mississippi River. Early in the summer of 1979, another creature was spotted near Westchester, in Cook County.

Then, later that summer, in August 1979, another significant encounter occurred just outside the town of West Frankfort in Franklin County. The witness, who was about twelve years old at the time, lived on the edge of town, not far from a wooded bottomland that was referred to as the Middle Fork. The swampy area, which had an abandoned railroad bed running through it, was often used as a dumping spot for junk and old appliances that the garbage service wouldn't pick up. The witness, who is referred to as "Joe" for privacy reasons, admitted to hearing reports of a Bigfoot-type creature in this area but never gave it much thought—until later, of course.

One afternoon, Joe was riding his bike along the rise of the abandoned rail line and after traveling some distance, realized that it was starting to get dark. He was headed back toward home when suddenly, two teenagers on a small motorcycle appeared around a bend in the trail and shouted to Joe that "a hobo was chasing them!" They passed by him quickly but Joe dismissed the story, believing the teenagers were teasing him. There was an encampment of hoboes in the woods but none of them had ever bothered the neighborhood children before.

As Joe rode along the trail, heading back to the residential area, he passed a spot where a number of washers and dryers had been dumped over the years. Behind one of the rusted appliances, which was laying on its side, he spotted the outline of what he first thought was a person. Joe stopped to take a closer look and the "person" stood up and looked back at him. The sun was behind the shape but Joe could see that it was quite tall and covered in hair, which was moving slightly in the breeze. He couldn't make out much detail in the face, thanks to the sun, but he could see a shine in its eyes, as well as a flattened nose and lips. He did not remember seeing ears on the wide head. The body was broad and heavily built and its arms were long. He did not remember smelling anything.

When the creature stood erect, it reached up with its right hand and grabbed a small tree that was close to it. As it grabbed hold of the tree, Joe recalled that it grunted slightly and then shook the tree. He did not get the impression that the monster was trying to be threatening, but it startled him nonetheless. He quickly started pedaling his bike again and rode off down the old railroad trail in the direction of his house. He only slowed down once to look back; when he did, he saw that the creature had climbed up onto the railroad bed and was looking down the trail toward him. It then turned slowly and walked into the trees as Joe rode towards home.

Joe told his parents and friends about the encounter but no one believed him at first. "They all thought I was nuts," he said, "until they started to hear other accounts, both before and after mine." After a few more stories from local people, the sightings faded away and the creature was never heard from again.

In July 1983, another mysterious creature raised its ugly head near Seneca in LaSalle County. Interestingly, Seneca would be the scene of more Bigfoot sightings a number of years later in the summer of 2005. In the 1983 event, two campers had a close encounter with something very out of the ordinary during an overnight trip.

One of the witnesses, who wanted only the name "John" to be used, was camping one night with his friend Chad. John's wife dropped them off in the woods and they hiked for some time into the forest before selecting a campsite and clearing out an area for their bedrolls and fire. They gathered up some firewood and as it got dark, they built a nice fire and made dinner. They had been relaxing for a few hours when, around 8:45 P.M., they heard something odd in the woods. They could clearly hear someone walking in the woods nearby, slowly circling their camp. It was a very dark night, with only a half moon, and they were unable to see very far into the forest. John would later state that it was "really hard to see even a silhouette of the trees with the skyline."

They could plainly hear something tromping about in the trees, though, walking steadily without a flashlight. Both of the men were experienced outdoorsmen and recognized that whatever was out there was walking on two legs. At one point, as the footsteps came closer to the camp, they caught a strong odor from the creature. John recalled: "It smelled a little bit like garbage, a little bit like musk cologne. It had a weird smell and one that I won't forget."

The creature continued to walk back and forth, circling the camp with apparent curiosity, for several hours. Needless to say, this caused a great amount of anxiety for the two campers. According to John, Chad started to panic after a while and demanded that they leave. John urged him to stay until morning. Not only was he curious about what was out in the forest but he was also not eager to enter the dark woods with whoever, or whatever, was watching them. However, as the footsteps started to sound more distant, John agreed to leave in the opposite direction. But almost as soon as Chad put out the fire, the monster rushed into their camp. As it entered the small clearing, John and Chad ducked down to hide.

"You could hear it breathing," John said. "Chad wanted to get up but I grabbed him and pulled him down . . . we started crawling out of there but it followed us out. I did see it circling back and forth and I could tell that it was quite a bit taller than me, and wider."

John spotted the creature in the clearing. Moments later, Chad saw it as they hurried out of the woods and onto the nearby road. He later claimed that it crossed the wide road in just three long strides. After that, it vanished into the forest, leaving two very shaken campers in its wake.

In October 1989, a sighting occurred in southern Illinois, just outside the small town of Sandoval. A local farmer was returning to his truck, which was parked about one mile northeast of the old Fairman meat-processing plant along Highway 51. He had been hunting for about three hours in some nearby woods and walked back through some bottoms toward his vehicle. As he entered a field near the top of a ravine, he heard a loud noise in the brush behind him. He glanced back down the hill but didn't see anything, so he kept walking. When he reached the other side of the field, he heard the noise again. This time, he crouched down behind some brush and waited to see what appeared.

As he looked back across the field, he saw a large creature that was also crouched down, as if also trying to hide. As first, he thought it was a bear, so he poked his head up to get a better look. A few moments later, the creature stood erect—it was definitely not a bear! Surprised, the witness stood up without thinking and saw the creature was looking right at him. It was dark brown and stood approximately seven feet tall. The hunter went on to say: "I could not see its face in great detail due to the distance, but I could make out a lighter color in the facial area . . . Its arms hung down to its side, and it had large thick legs."

The hunter stood very still and, apparently copying the man's movements, the creature stood just as still. Then, suddenly, it made a low, loud grunt, waved its left arm in the air, and then turned back toward the trees and disappeared into the woods.

"At that point," the witness stated, "I was scared enough not to cross back over the field and pursue it, or even try to see it again. I went straight to my vehicle and left the area."

There were no other reports of a creature in the area.

Another startling creature encounter, this time with a lone driver, occurred in September 1999 in Henry County, just north of Kewanee. The witness was coming home late one evening after working second shift at a nearby factory. He had been working that same shift, which ended around 2:00 A.M., for more than six years and was used to the drive, the roads, and the late hour.

He added: "I had encountered lots of different animals on those roads. And I do know the difference in the many species of animal life in this area. I grew up here and have always spent time in the woods, fishing and just tracking . . . However, on this night, I saw something completely out of place."

He was driving down a side road that led over Mud Creek to his house, where there are two bends in the road just before the bridge. "I am always careful there as that's where deer like to walk through," he said.

The witness drove around the first curve and onto about two hundred feet of straight road before the curve to the right. His headlights lit up the curve, along with a stretch of fence and cornfield. That was when he saw something on the other side of the fence. He remembered that he observed it for about five or six seconds as he drove directly toward it, getting a good look at the thing.

The creature was standing on two legs, leaning against the fence at the edge of the cornfield with both its upper arms bent. Because of the height of the fence, the witness estimated the monster to be around seven-and-a-half feet tall. Although it was hard to tell because it was covered with a thick layer of dark hair, he estimated its weight to be around to at least three hundred and fifty pounds. The creature's chest appeared to be bare, although he could not see below its upper torso behind the fence. The monster's head was large and its face was sort of "smashed and reminded me of how a bulldog looks," he said. He also added that he got the distinct impression that the creature was old, or at least "had some age to it."

The driver was almost to the second curve in the road when the monster began to run, on two legs, into the cornfield, which led to some woods to the west. "There was perhaps another three hundred feet to the bridge from that curve," the witness remembered. "By the time I reached it, I had goose bumps the size of eggs and my hair, what's left of it, was trying to stand up."

An unconnected northern Illinois encounter occurred near Essex in July 2000. One night, Andrew Souligne of Union Hill and his daughter, Crissy, were driving on a sand road that runs past an old graveyard just east of town when a large, hairy shape walked out in front of the car. The creature froze in the headlights and turned towards the car, apparently stunned by the bright lights from the vehicle. Souligne and his daughter were likewise shocked, and he immediately put the car into reverse to back away from the monster. Moments later, the monster loped into the woods and vanished. "I'm not saying that it was Bigfoot," Souligne stated several years later. "I don't know exactly what it was. I guess you would say a man-creature . . . almost a hairy man, like an animal."

Another possible Bigfoot encounter occurred near Alton during the weekend of May 15 and 16, 2004, at a place called Maple Island. This remote and heavily wooded spot is located just across the Mississippi River in a wildlife preserve and is a popular spot for bird watchers, fishermen, and outdoor enthusiasts. According to the witness, he and his nephew and brother-in-law were on a fishing trip near the Alton dam when their sighting took place.

The weird events began just as they arrived at the nearby boat ramp and started preparing to launch their boat. The sun had not yet come up and the woods around the river were dark. As they were preparing to put the boat into the water, another fisherman hurried over and told them that a "crazy person" was throwing rocks at him from the woods. The man had been fishing near the boat ramp and no one else could be seen in the surrounding parking lot. The woods where the rocks were coming from were located on the other side of a small creek, which meant that the stones had to have been thrown from at least one hundred feet away. He advised the men not to launch their boat because it was possible that they could be hurt. Some of the rocks, he explained, were large enough to have seriously injured him.

Curious, one of the other men got a powerful spotlight from the truck and aimed it toward the trees. To his surprise, he saw a set of bluish-white eyes looking back at him! As the light hit the figure, the eyes turned away and disappeared. Before the man could call out about what he had seen, the younger nephew said that he had seen them, too. Whatever had been there, it was gone, the men decided, and they launched the boat and continued their fishing trip without incident.

The following day, the witness returned to the site with his brother. They brought cameras along with them and again prepared to launch their boat. As they were sitting on the curb talking, then were shocked when a small rock hit the boat. The witness again grabbed his spotlight and illuminated the woods with it. They saw nothing, but just then, a large rock crashed to the ground next to them. They quickly launched the boat with no further problems but they were convinced that something was out there in the woods.

Throughout the spring and summer of 2005, Bigfoot—if the reports could be believed—apparently returned to the area around Seneca, which is located about seventy miles southwest of Chicago. For several months, the area outside of town along DuPont Road became the epicenter of the sightings. A number of reports came from this heavily wooded area, which according to local residents was well-known for sightings dating back nearly forty years. Longtime residents referred to the creature as the "DuPont Monster." It had always been regarded as nothing more than an urban legend by most people but, for those who encountered it, the creature was anything but a myth.

A local man, who gave his name as "Tom" for privacy reasons, first spotted the creature on June 2, 2005. He returned to the scene of the sighting about one week later with a friend and the friend's son to show them where he had seen a hulking beast alongside a bend in the road. They parked their car about thirty feet from the curve and got out so that Tom could show them the site. As they were talking, Tom and his friend "John" heard a loud commotion out in the woods. They peered down into the woods to see what was out there and John was the first one to see the silhouette of something large and dark. He called Tom over and pointed out what he saw. Tom strained to see what his friend was trying to point out until suddenly, both of the men saw the arm of the shape move to the side. Excited, Tom climbed onto the hood of his car to get a better look; from that vantage point he could plainly see the majority of a dark body. The creature, which was similar to the Bigfoot shape that he had seen a week earlier, was standing motionless against a tree, apparently hoping to avoid the men's scrutiny.

A moment later, Tom was shocked to see movement a dozen or so feet away from the creature. He looked over and saw another hairy figure, smaller than the first one, walking slowly through the stand of trees. He called out to his friend and John also saw the second creature. Without thinking, Tom jumped down from the car and ran into the woods in the direction of the smaller monster. Almost as soon as he started to run, crashing through the underbrush, the second figure also began to run, dashing in the opposite direction. He never caught up to it. The creature managed to stay ahead of him and quickly disappeared. Neither he nor John saw what became of the first monster after the chase. It had simply melted into the forest and vanished.

Another Seneca encounter occurred about three weeks later on June 28. This time, a local resident was traveling near DuPont Road and spotted a creature dart across in front of his car. "Rich" was coming home from work around 9:30 P.M. As he turned onto the road he had to slam on his brakes when a large figure came out of the woods to the right of his vehicle. The creature, which Rich described as being "about seven feet tall and covered with dark hair," lurched forward and then stopped, as if surprised to see the automobile. Rich recalled that the creature hesitated for a moment and then sprinted across the road and disappeared into the woods on the other side.

"It seemed like it was scared," he remembered, "or at least surprised by the fact that I was there."

Rich, himself startled, pulled over to the side of the road and took a moment to catch his breath. He got out of the car and retrieved a flashlight from the trunk and debated for a moment about following the trail the creature had cut through the trees. One glance at the dark woods, however, made him decide against this plan.

A few weeks later, on the afternoon of July 20, a couple traveling through the area on a visit to relatives had another encounter with a Seneca Bigfoot. Paul and Stacy Dearing were traveling from Morris to Seneca and had turned off on a side road, following directions from one of Paul's cousins. They ended up taking a wrong turn and became slightly lost. After making a few wrong turns, Paul stopped the car and tried to get a signal on his mobile phone so that he could call his cousin and see where to go next. He had trouble getting a good signal, but after a couple of failed attempts, he managed to connect with his cousin. He had just finished jotting down some additional directions and had put the automobile into gear when Stacy let out a loud gasp.

Paul followed his wife's gaze and saw what she was looking at. No more than twenty yards away from the car, a large, black, hulking shape squatted at the edge of the woods. The creature was a few feet into a clearing that started at the edge of the road and extended some distance to the forest. The creature seemed not to notice their vehicle and was apparently digging at something in the ground. Both Paul and Stacy got a good look at it in the bright afternoon sunshine. It was very large and thick with wide shoulders and heavy legs. It was covered in heavy black fur that "was filled with stickers and burrs, like it had been rolling around in the weeds."

A couple moments later, the beast looked up and spotted the car and its staring human occupants, stood, and then began quickly walking away from them toward the trees. The monster walked forward but looked back over its shoulder at them as it hurried away. The creature pushed aside a few small trees and then pressed into the forest, quickly disappearing from sight. Neither Paul nor Stacy had any intention of going after it. After quickly deciding that both of them had just seen the same thing, they drove away and went straight to their cousin's house, where they told their family what they had seen.

Although skeptical at first, the family members soon realized they were serious and became convinced that Paul and Stacy had actually seen something. Paul took his cousin back to the spot the next afternoon and while they didn't find any footprints, they did find a small hole that had been dug in the ground at the spot where the creature had been sitting.

"Whatever it was, it was real," Stacy stated firmly. "There is something out there in those woods."

The Big Muddy Monster

southern Illinois, with its thick forests, open fields, rocky cliffs and canyons, and often sparse population, seems to have a weirdness about it that one might not find in the cities and more crowded areas in other parts of the state. The Shawnee National Forest covers miles and miles of territory in the southernmost portion of the region. The acres of forest seem almost untouched by man, and some believe that strange things occasionally walk here, usually—but not always—unseen by human eyes.

One such creature, a monster that wreaked havoc in the small southern Illinois town of Murphysboro, was first seen around midnight on Monday, June 25, 1973. On that humid and steamy night, a young couple, Randy Needham and Judy Johnson, were parked near a boat ramp along the Big Muddy River near Murphysboro. The evening had been quiet until a strange, roaring cry shattered the stillness of the night. It came from the nearby woods and both Randy and Judy looked up to see a huge shape lumbering toward them from the shadows. Whatever the thing was, it walked on two legs and continued to make the horrible sound. They later described the noise as "something not human."

According to their account, the monster was about seven feet tall and covered with matted, whitish hair. The "fur" was streaked liberally with mud from the river. As it lurched toward them, the tone of the creature's cry began to change, alarming them even further. When the creature approached to within twenty feet of them, they quickly left the scene. They went directly to the Murphysboro police station and reported their bloodcurdling encounter.

"They were absolutely terrified," former police chief Ron Manwaring recalled in 2003, the thirtieth anniversary of the sightings. The retired officer agreed to be interviewed about the case and recounted all he could recall about what happened. "I'm convinced that they saw something that night . . . I can't tell you what it was that they saw, whether it was a bear or something else. But something was definitely there."

A short time later, officers Meryl Lindsay and Jimmie Nash returned to the area and surveyed the scene. Although skeptical, they were surprised to find that a number of footprints had been left in the mud. The footprints were "approximately ten to twelve inches long and approximately three inches wide," according to their report. At 2:00 A.M., Nash, Lindsay, a Jackson County sheriff's deputy named Bob Scott, and Randy Needham returned to the scene again. This time, they discovered more tracks and Lindsay left to get a camera. The others followed the new footprints, tracing their path along the river.

Suddenly, the creature's terrifying scream was heard again, coming from the woods about one hundred yards away. The men didn't wait to see if they could spot the monster. Instead, they made a quick retreat to the patrol car. Needham later recalled that the sheriff's deputy was so scared that he dropped his gun into the mud. After waiting in the darkness for a little while, they got back out again and spent the rest of the night trying to track down a splashing sound they heard in the distance. Things quieted down after daylight, but the next night, the creature was back.

The first to see the monster on the second evening was a four-year-old boy named Christian Baril, who told his parents that he saw a "big white ghost in the yard." They didn't believe him, but when Randy Creath and Cheryl Ray saw an identical monster in a neighboring yard just ten minutes later, Christian's parents—and the police—quickly reconsidered the little boy's statement.

Randy and Cheryl spotted the monster at about 10:30 P.M. while sitting on the back porch of the Ray house. They heard the sound of something moving in the woods near the river and then spotted the mud-streaked, white creature staring at them with glowing pink eyes. Cheryl would later insist that the eyes were actually glowing and were not reflecting light from some other source. They estimated that it weighed at least three hundred and fifty pounds, stood seven feet tall, and had a roundish head and long arms like an ape's. Cheryl turned on the porch light and Randy went for a closer look. The creature seemed unconcerned and finally ambled off into the woods. Investigators would later find a trail of broken tree branches and crushed undergrowth, along with a number of large footprints. They also noticed a strong odor left in the monster's wake, which faded away after a few minutes.

Officer Nash and Police Chief Manwaring soon arrived at the scene. They brought with them a local man named Jerry Nellis, who had a trained German shepherd that was often used by the police department as an attack dog and for searching buildings and tracking suspects. The dog was immediately put on the trail of the monster. He followed what appeared to be a slimy path through the weeds and then managed to track the creature through the woods and down a hill to a small pond. Eventually, the trees and undergrowth became too thick for the dog to continue and it was thrown off the track just moments after almost pulling its handler down a steep embankment. The officers began searching the area with flashlights and the dog began sniffing near the trees, hoping to pick up the scent again. He then set off toward an abandoned barn, but refused to go inside. In fact, the animal began barking and shaking with fear.

Nellis called the two officers over and they opened the barn and went inside. After a few moments, they realized that it was empty. The three men were puzzled. The dog had been trained to search buildings and Nellis could not explain why it had refused to enter the barn. A short time later, the search was called off for the night.

The "Mud Monster," as the beast came to be known, was reported two more times that summer. On the night of July 4, traveling carnival workers stated that they spotted the creature disturbing some Shetland ponies that were being used for the holiday celebration at Riverside Park. This report actually came in on July 7 because the carnival owner was concerned that the sighting might scare away potential holiday customers. However, he did tell the police that several of his workers noticed the ponies attempting to break loose from the trees where they had been tied up for the night. According to the police report, the workers described the monster as being seven to eight feet tall with light brown hair all over its body. It stood erect on two legs and weighed at least three hundred to four hundred pounds. The creature stood very close to the ponies and while it seemed curious, it did not advance on them or threaten them in any way.

Then, on July 7, Mrs. Nedra Green heard a screaming sound coming from a shed on her rural farm. She did not go out to investigate but the description of the cries matched the description given by Randy Needham, Judy Johnson, and the police officers who also heard it.

As the story leaked out, it turned up in the newspapers, got posted to the wire services, and soon made national headlines. Even the *New York Times* sent a reporter to investigate. The story of the Big Muddy Monster was reported all around the world and soon letters came pouring into the Murphysboro Police Department from all over the country and even from as far away as South Africa. Researchers, curiosity-seekers, and even scientists were pleading with the local authorities to release more information.

They received letters from hunters and trappers who offered to track down the monster and kill it or capture it. Two men from Oregon offered to do the job and wrote that they "would be willing to take on this adventure at only the cost of expenses and materials for doing so." Some wrote suggesting that the police use bait to snare the creature. A Florida man suggested, "Why don't you put bread and cheese and eggs out for your creature? You would have a splendid attraction if you could have it in a little hut, to show people."

Assistant professor Leigh Van Valen, from the University of Chicago's biology department, also wrote a letter to Chief Manwaring. "I have heard of your creature," the letter stated, "which could be of considerable scientific interest. There have been many reports of such animals but no real specimens have been available for scientific study." Professor Van Valen went on to explain how the creature, if circumstances required shooting it, should be properly embalmed or "preserved in good condition." The professor agreed to cover the necessary expenses to procure the monster for scientific study; it wouldn't matter, though, for the monster never returned to Murphysboro.

There was only one other sighting that could have possibly been the creature and it occurred in the fall of that same year, a number of miles southwest of town, near the Mississippi River. A local truck driver told police that he saw a monster that resembled the Murphysboro creature along the edge of the road. It vanished before he could get a good look at it, but it did leave behind a number of large tracks in the mud. The authorities made casts of the impressions but they were unable to determine if they matched the previous footprints or were the work of a prankster. After that one last hurrah, the Big Muddy Monster simply faded away. As far as we know, it disappeared without a trace after that.

So what was the Murphysboro Mud Monster? Local authorities admitted that they didn't know and after almost forty years, no one has ever come forward with a logical explanation for the sightings. One of the police officers involved in the case said, "A lot of things in life are unexplained and this is another one. We don't know what the creature is, but we do believe what these people saw was real."

Randy Needham, one of the first people to see the monster, agreed in an interview. "It would be kind of naïve for us to think that we know everything that's out there," he said. He went on to admit that he never goes into the woods at night, and if he enters the woods in the daytime, "I always look for a way out in case I need to leave fast."

The Enfield Horror

The year 1973 was a strange one in Illinois. For some reason, it was a year that saw an unusually high number of encounters with things that simply defied explanation, from manlike monsters to giant birds. However, there are few reports stranger than those that came from the small southern Illinois town of Enfield that spring. The tiny community became the scene of a bizarre string of happenings that are still remembered today as some of the strangest events to ever occur in Illinois.

Henry McDaniel of Enfield almost became the first man to be arrested because of what was soon known as the "Enfield

Horror." White County Sheriff Roy Poshard Jr. threatened to lock up McDaniel for telling folks about the weird events that he claimed took place at his home on April 25, 1973. Convinced the man was a heavy drinker, the sheriff wanted to shut McDaniel up and keep him from starting a panic. If even a portion of what he was saying was true, then Enfield would soon be in an uproar.

Despite the sheriff's threats, McDaniel stuck by his story and he became the first to report what would turn into a nightmare for the little town. McDaniel claimed that he was at home on the evening of April 25 when he heard something scratching at his front door. When he opened it, he was stunned by the sight of some sort of creature on his porch. He stated that "it had three legs on it, a short body, two little short arms coming out of its breast area, and two pink eyes as big as flashlights. It stood four-and-a-half to five feet tall and was grayish-colored. It was trying to get into the house."

McDaniel scrambled backward and slammed the door shut. He quickly retrieved his pistol, ran back to the front room, kicked opened the door, and opened fire. The creature was still lurking on the porch and he knew that he hit it with the first shot. The monster "hissed like a wildcat" and scampered away, covering seventy-five feet in three jumps. It disappeared into the brush along the railroad tracks near his house. McDaniel then called the police and reported the event. Despite their skepticism, officers responded, likely because of the gunshots that McDaniel admitted had taken place. Several Illinois state troopers also answered the call and found tracks "like those of a dog, except they had six toe pads." The tracks were measured and two of them were four inches across and the third was slightly smaller.

As it turned out, McDaniel was not the first to see the creature. A young boy, Greg Garrett, who lived just behind McDaniel, had been playing in his yard about a half hour before the ominous knocking on McDaniel's door. He claimed that the creature had emerged from the shadows and "attacked" him. The monster had merely stomped up and down on the boy's feet but its misshapen, and apparently sharp, feet tore the boy's tennis shoes to shreds. Greg managed to escape from the weird monster and he ran into the house, crying hysterically.

On May 6, McDaniel was awakened in the middle of the night by howling neighborhood dogs. He looked out his front door and saw the monster again. It was standing out near the railroad tracks. He was able to see the creature by the glow of a pole light in his yard. He showed remarkable restraint by not immediately going for his gun again. "I didn't shoot at it or anything," McDaniel reported. "It started on down the railroad track. It wasn't in a hurry or anything."

McDaniel's reports soon brought publicity to Enfield and prompted the threats from the county sheriff, but it was too late. Soon, hordes of curiosity-seekers, reporters, and researchers descended on the town. Among the "monster hunters" were five young men who were arrested by Deputy Sheriff Jim Clark as "threats to public safety" and for hunting violations. This was after they had opened fire on a gray, hairy thing that they had seen in some underbrush on May 8. Two of the men thought they had hit it, but it sped off, moving faster than a man could. The police confiscated the men's rifles and locked them up temporarily. Apparently, shooting up the streets of Enfield was frowned upon by the police.

One more credible witness to the monster was Rick Rainbow, who was then the news director of radio station WWKI in Kokomo, Indiana. He and three other people spotted the monster near an abandoned house, just a short distance from McDaniel's place. They didn't get much of a look at it as it was running away from them, but they later described it as about five feet tall, gray, and stooped over. Rainbow did manage to tape-record its cry, though. The wailing was also heard by others who came to try and track down the creature, including Loren Coleman, who is now an eminent cryptozoologist. At the time, he was an anthropology and zoology student at the University of Illinois who was drawn to Enfield by the publicity generated by the monster sightings. Coleman and others heard the wails near the railroad tracks that were close to the McDaniel home.

A short time later, the sightings ended as abruptly as they began. What plagued the residents of Enfield? No one knows, even to this day. No attempt was ever made by the authorities to debunk the case and no one ever suggested what this creature could have been—aside from some unknown beast that came from nowhere and vanished back to the same place.

Some have surmised that the entire affair was nothing more than an elaborate hoax, but this fails to explain the number of witnesses and the eerie recordings that were captured. Others believe the monster may have been connected to UFO activity that was also reported in the general area at the time, but little documentation exists about such activity and whether or not any of it was near Enfield.

I visited Enfield in the summer of 2004 and spoke to a number of people about their memories of April and May 1973. Many that I spoke with had never heard of the encounters at all, but several others spoke guardedly of that spring, usually talking in a low voice as if they didn't want anyone else to hear what they were saying. An older woman that I met in one of the local gas stations explained that most people were embarrassed to talk about what had occurred. "Things were in such an uproar around here at the time," she said. "There were people coming into town looking for monsters. It was all really kind of silly considering that hardly anyone saw the thing anyway. We were all locking our doors at night, though, and not letting the kids play outside after dark. Thinking back, we probably overreacted, but most everyone I knew was pretty scared."

What did she think the thing was?

"No idea," she replied, "and I can't even say for sure that it was real. I never saw anything and don't know anyone who did. I had a neighbor who heard some weird noises one night but that could have been a stray dog, I don't know. I've got no idea what that thing could have been—but I sure wouldn't have wanted it scratching on my door in the middle of the night."

So, what was the monster that prowled the streets and alleys of this small town? The only thing that we know for sure about the Enfield Horror is that it was an enigma and that it remains so today.

Mysterious Menagerie of Panthers, Lions, and Kangaroos

Despite the fact that mountain lions have been extinct in Illinois for many years, reports of "phantom" animals continue to emerge from time to time. Many of these reports seem to be centered in central and southern Illinois. Many old pioneer records speak of the dangers of living on the prairies and tell of "panthers" being one of the greatest threats to their lives. As time passed, though, the mountain lion population vanished in the late nineteenth century and officials will quickly say that there are no big cats left in Illinois. So why do these big cat sightings continue? Strangest of all, why do many of the sightings involve black panthers—a breed of big cat that, unlike mountain lions, had never been known to exist in Illinois, or even North America, at all?

The stories of black panthers in Illinois date back a number of decades. There are tales of wild cats screaming in the night, mysterious black shapes that suddenly appear in the headlights of passing automobiles, and sleek, feline shapes that vanish into open fields. There have been firsthand accounts of muddy footprints as big as a man's fist and mysterious tracks that leave us with no other explanation than to consider the idea that monstrous cats still prowl the region. But why do they remain—and stranger still, how did they get here in the first place?

During the 1950s and 1960s, reports of panthers turned up almost monthly. Some of them were reported in local newspapers and many weren't, the witnesses fearing scorn and ridicule. Legends and folklore attributed the appearance of big cats to wrecked circus trains and escapees from local zoos, but these stories could seldom be found to have any basis in truth. What we do know is that the panthers have appeared at regular intervals and then disappeared without a trace. A hunter told me that in 1958 he took a shot at one of the beasts and, like scores of others across the country, was sure that he wounded it. He found neither a body nor a blood trail.

Are these black panthers real animals or figments of the imagination? That is, of course, up to the reader to decide, but there are many who believe the stories to be true. In DeKalb County in 1990, law enforcement officials blamed a big cat for the slaughter of local farm animals. Security staff at Fort Sheridan, on Chicago's North Shore, chased down numerous big cat sightings in 1993. A family outside of Decatur found dozens of huge feline tracks around their farm in the fall of 1994 but thought little of it until their dog was attacked and the wounds on the animal's throat and shoulder could not be spanned by his owner's hand. A number of sightings, along with the discovery of some tracks, took place along Macoupin Creek near Carlinville in 2003 and 2004. And while big cats were allegedly driven out of Lake County many years ago, more than fifty people reported sightings of panthers in 2009 alone.

The sightings continue to take place in spite of the fact that Illinois has not officially been home to a species of big cat for many years. When they are reported, the standard response seems to be that the mystery cats are domesticated animals that somehow escaped from, or were released by, their owners. Officials from the Illinois Department of Natural Resources maintain that they have never been able to confirm the existence of panthers and cougars in the area, despite the numerous reports. "If there are cougars in Illinois, they must have been released by someone or escaped from someone," said Tim Schweizer, IDNR spokesman. "We know of no instances of wild cougars in Illinois." Although Schweizer said the agency does receive calls from "time to time," the staff has been unable to confirm the reports.

State officials believe that many, even most, of the big cat sightings can be attributed to poor eyesight, confusion, and overactive imaginations. They don't bother to investigate the claims of Illinois panthers but other researchers do go to the trouble. John Lutz of the Eastern Puma Research Network reports that a number of big cat sightings have occurred recently in Illinois. These sightings are usually of mountain lions that are tan or chocolate in color.

As mentioned, though, of all of the big cat sightings that occur in Illinois, the strangest are those of black panthers. The main reason for this is that these types of cats are not, and have never been, indigenous to North America. Black pumas are known in South America, which continues to raise the possibility that the big cats that are seen may be released or escaped exotic pets. Lutz believes that some reports of black panthers can be traced to imported animals released by their owners or cats that escaped off of circus trains, but not all of them. He told me that, "State and federal wildlife officials, and a few independent researchers of other groups, claim black panthers or leopards have escaped from circus locations. They could explain some of the big cats in this manner but there aren't that many circus trains to have derailed to account for the total number of black panther sightings that exist." Lutz even cited evidence that contradicts the claims of state officials. "One of our independent researchers in Illinois got a photo of a large black cat walking away from his camera location," he claimed. "So, there is documented evidence of black panthers in Illinois, which contradicts the claims of state officials."

If the state's explanations were true in some cases, would it really explain the numerous sightings that occur in Illinois, dating back several decades? There would have to be as many people keeping black panthers in their homes as cocker spaniels if this was true. Or could the panthers be wandering animals that managed to migrate to the north from their natural habitats? Possibly, but wouldn't such a large number of animals be seen as they traveled such a long distance?

Who can say? That just seems to be part of the mystery of Illinois's weird history of big cats.

While the reader may have some doubts about the existence of black panthers in Illinois, I don't share them. I believe that Illinois's black panthers are real and that they are often seen by ordinary and quite rational people. One black panther sighting is a part of my family folklore. One night, in the fall of 1960, my stepfather's mother sighted a panther crossing the road in front of her car. The sighting took place just east of Moweaqua, Illinois, and my family remembers the event quite distinctly. To this day, my stepfather can take me right to the spot where his mother's sighting occurred.

But this secondhand story was not what really convinced me. I became interested in reports of phantom cats in the spring of 1984 after I spotted one of my own! I was walking in the woods about a mile from my home near Moweaqua when I was startled by the sound of something running in the nearby underbrush. I looked up quickly and saw the unmistakable shape of a huge black cat streaking through the trees. I chased after it for a short distance, never really considering what I thought I was going to do if I caught up to it, but the cat was gone. The animal vanished but I knew what I had seen. There was no question that it had been a black panther. I was sure about the color and the size and I had not confused it with some other animal. I was very familiar with the woods and with the wildlife that could be found there. I firmly believe that I saw a black panther that day in the forest, whether science accepts the idea or not.

Needless to say, this sparked my interest and I began to learn that panther sightings were frequent in wooded areas near lakes and rivers in Illinois. Nearby Decatur was a hotspot for sightings that dated back more than a century. In the years following World War I, the river bottoms near Faries Park in Decatur had been cleared and a tree was found bearing the carved words "I killed a panther 1851."

Historical records of central Illinois told many other stories, as well. Frontier chronicler Eliza Farnham reported that panthers were often seen in the forests along the creek bottoms in Tazewell County where she lived in the 1840s. The cats largely avoided the human population of the time but when they did meet, the results were usually bloody. One story from the annals of pioneer life told of a young man who was snatched off the back of his horse, killed, and partially devoured by a large panther. A man named William Huffmaster, who lived on Lick Creek in Sangamon County, helped a neighbor tree a panther one day. When the neighbor left to fetch a gun, Huffmaster, with the help of his hunting dogs, caught the animal and clubbed it to death.

The stories appeared here and there in history books and in family accounts, but by the 1950s, newspaper reporters were on the scent of the strange stories. On September 15, 1955, the *Decatur Review* reported that several residents on the east side of Lake Decatur, near Rea's Bridge, reported to authorities that they had seen a black panther. On September 13, a woman claimed to have seen the animal along Old Sangamon Road and that sighting was followed the next night by another, reported by two truck drivers near Rea's Bridge. The cat was described as being low-slung and jet-black in color with gleaming eyes. In addition to the sightings, a number of people who lived in the neighborhood told Macon County sheriff's deputies that they had been hearing an animal's screams during the night. The reports continued to come in for the next few weeks and while the sightings were taken seriously, officials could not be sure that the animal was actually a panther, especially after several of the sightings turned out to be nothing more than large dogs.

On October 26, however, a little over a month after the Rea's Bridge sightings, a Decatur game warden named Paul G. Myers confirmed the fact that the animal was indeed a black panther. He not only saw the beast, but also wounded it, near the Coulter's Mill area of the Sangamon River bottoms.

Myers was checking on some duck hunters and was standing near a thicket when he heard an animal squeal. He thought that it might be a rabbit that had been caught by a fox. When he walked over to the thicket, he was stunned to see that it was a panther eating the rabbit. Myers was armed with his service revolver, which he quickly aimed and shot at the animal. The panther jumped and ran into the woods. Myers followed its course using his field glasses and after a short dash, the animal dropped down and started licking its flank where the game warden believed he had hit it. He described the panther as being black, standing two feet tall at the shoulders, and having a body length of four or five feet. Myers started toward the animal again but this time when it ran, it vanished into the forest. He returned to the area a short time later to make an intensive search, but the panther was never found.

The next Decatur sighting occurred on June 30, 1963, and appeared under the headline "Big Cat Attacks Man" in the local newspaper. An early-morning telephone call to the police brought a number of officers to the home of George W. Davidson on Summit Avenue. Davidson had been awakened around 3:00 A.M. by barking from a number of dogs in the neighborhood. He went outside, armed with a shotgun, and began searching for the source of the commotion. There had been rumors circulating that a panther had been seen in the area, but Davidson believed that he was well-armed to deal with the beast if it was nearby. He had just walked into his backyard when he saw a large cat leap over a five-foot fence and disappear into a wooded area behind the house. Davidson went into the thicket and the cat leapt at him from the trees. He was knocked to the ground by the animal but it ran off, leaving him with only minor cuts and scratches. Mrs. Davidson, who had remained in the house, watching the excitement, fainted when the panther jumped onto her husband. Davidson quickly recovered and managed to fire several shots at the animal and told police officers that he was pretty sure that he had wounded it. However, no sign of the panther was ever found, save for a few fresh tracks, and it vanished from the area.

Almost exactly two years later, on June 24, 1965, a woman who lived along Faries Parkway in Decatur reported that she saw a large, black panther "as tall as the headlights on a car." She was turning into her driveway and the animal darted in front of the car and ran quickly away. Sheriff's deputies and an Illinois state trooper investigated the scene but were unable to find anything but a large, possibly feline print that measured about four inches across. Reports followed of nocturnal animal screams in the area; three days later, on the south side of the city, a black panther surprised three children in Lincoln Park. The children ran away in a panic and the big cat helped itself to their sack lunches before vanishing back into the woods.

Macon County Sheriff's deputies responded to another call in late June 1967 when Anthony J. Viccone reported seeing a big cat just south of Decatur. The cat was seen near his home, which was about one-third of a mile east of South Franklin Street Road and close to Elwin. He described the panther as looking exactly like a mountain lion and weighing about one hundred seventy-five pounds. Viccone, originally from the West Coast, had hunted for many years in the mountains and was familiar with the appearance of mountain lions. He had called the authorities after becoming concerned about children playing in the area. Authorities admitted that they had taken many reports of big cats in the area. "We have seen tracks and other evidence," they said, "but have never gotten close enough to the animal to determine what type of cat it is."

In June of 1970, an employee of the Macon Seed Company, located west of Decatur, saw a large, black cat that he said resembled a cougar. A game warden announced two days later that the animal seen near the seed company was a beaver. One has to wonder what this "beaver" looked like, as the seed company employees reported that it left behind large feline paw prints.

Later that same year, in December, the Clarence Runyon family of Decatur reported seeing a large panther and its cub in a field outside of town. They believed the animal might have been the reason why forty chickens had vanished from their farm over the summer months. Several of the Runyons' neighbors had also seen the panthers and heard them scream-ing. On December 10, twenty-two-year-old Karen Thrall, the Runyons' oldest daughter, saw the two cats in a field near the house. She stated that the panther seemed to be fully grown and the cub was about the size of a small dog. Later that evening, she and the rest of the family watched with binocu-lars as the cats lounged and walked around the same field. Officials from the Department of Conservation investigated the case and noted that the tracks left behind had definitely been made by a panther. They planned to shoot the animals when they caught them, but the panthers were never seen again.

In 1976, another black panther was sighted in southern Macon County and a man named Louis Jockisch managed to make an audio recording of the cat's cries. Later that same year, a Macon County sheriff's deputy reported seeing a large catlike animal just west of Decatur. The cat slipped and fell as it ducked out of the way of the officer's car. The cat then jumped a fence and ran into a cornfield. The deputy fired off several shots but didn't believe that he had hit the cat. That fall, several more sightings were reported by residents of the area.

During the summer of 1980, what was believed to be a black panther was reported prowling around a small farm on the Mechanicsburg Blacktop, just east of Springfield. Amy Butler, who lived on the farm with her parents and grandparents, contacted me about the series of incidents that happened that year. Their neighbor at the time was a man named Paul Fink, who kept sheep in a pasture right next to the farmhouse. On three occasions early in the summer, three of his sheep were literally torn apart and partially eaten in the middle of the night. The first time this happened, Amy and her parents were fishing in the nearby Sangamon River and heard what sounded like a woman screaming in the distance. They became unnerved and decide to cut short that afternoon's fishing trip.

After the second sheep killing, Mr. Fink, Amy's father, her grandfather, and a cousin decided to take guns and stake out the pasture at night to try and catch whatever was killing the animals. They climbed onto the roof of the Fink barn and waited up there until about 3:00 A.M. Moments later, they saw something coming across the pasture from the river. As it entered the pasture, the men opened fire. They scared it away but before it vanished, all of them managed to get a good look at it. "What they claimed to see," Amy told me some years later, "was definitely a black panther."

The animal was described as being about four feet long with an extended, feline tail; it was two feet high at the shoulder and jet-black in color. The men searched for the animal until daybreak but could never find any sign of it, aside from a few tracks in the mud. Even though they were sure that they had hit it with their initial volley, there was no trace of blood and they found no wounded or dead cat. The panther returned on one additional occasion, killing and eating another Fink sheep, but was never seen again. The tracks continued to appear around the farm for a short time afterward, but then they also vanished.

The panthers are not confined to just central Illinois. In September 1960, an Alton man reported that he saw a black panther along a back road near Grafton. He stated that it stood almost as high as the hood of his car and when he slammed on the brakes, it ran off into the woods. Another witness told me of a sighting that occurred just outside of Alton in 1971. He was also driving when the animal suddenly crossed the road in front of him. The cat slipped as it was trying to get out of the way of the car and then jumped a fence and vanished into a field. The man told me that later that fall, a number of neighbors who lived in the area also reported seeing the panther.

In the summer of 1985, a Jersey County woman told me of the problems that she had keeping food for her dogs. She had a number of animals and kept them in a shaded area of the yard at the edge of her property. The dogs had two kennels that they shared and at night were always kept chained up. In June of that year, the woman and her husband began to hear strange sounds coming from a wooded area near their property. They were unable to identify the sounds at first, which she described as a screaming noise, but soon realized that it was a panther or a big cat. She normally fed her dogs each evening, often with table scraps, and in the morning she started to find huge paw prints in the dirt around the kennels.

The dogs could always be found huddling inside and she had to coax them to come out. The paw prints they found were always around the food dishes that had been put out for the dogs and they realized that whatever was in the woods—and leaving those massive tracks behind—was eating the food. After a few mornings of finding the tracks, the woman began locking the dogs in the garage at night. With its food source cut off, whatever was out in the woods apparently moved on and the screams in the night stopped.

Black panther sightings have continued to be a part of the mysterious folklore—and reality—of southern Illinois and the sightings still continue today. In September 1998, a cougar was repeatedly sighted near Edwardsville. While authorities found no trace of the animal, which was first seen on the playground of the LeClaire School, state wildlife officials admitted that it was the third report of a cougar near the city that year. Customers and employees of the New You Salon on Franklin Avenue also reported the cat. Five people told police that they had seen the animal inside the fence around the Illinois Power natural gas monitoring station, just northeast of the intersection of Franklin and Madison Avenues. One of the hair salon customers, a firefighter, was the first to spot the animal and he called the police. A witness stated that the cat was huge and had a long and extremely thick tail. Police officers, while stating that they took the reports seriously, dismissed them as nothing more than reports of a "tomcat" in the neighborhood. Brenda Edgeworth, the owner of the hair salon, went on record to say, "That was not a cat. I have seen some large house cats before. It was larger than that."

The other Edwardsville sightings had taken place in the spring of 1998. One cougar had been seen near the Southern Illinois University campus and another near Dunlap Lake. An additional sighting had also taken place near Collinsville. State wildlife officials who investigated the reports and searched the areas stated (predictably) that they had found no evidence of panthers.

Black panther sightings returned to the central part of the state in April 1999. Bev and Mike Ray, who lived in the country near Clarksdale, about five miles south of Taylorville, began spotting a black panther in the yard during the early morning hours, just after dawn. Bev Ray spotted the animal first. "It was jet black, and it was just calmly walking along, not running or anything. And it was big," she recalled. "I saw it from less than a few hundred feet away and it was really, really big. It walked through my yard and disappeared into some timber nearby." Following the first sighting, the Rays began to find large prints around their property, which is also home to a large menagerie of dogs, cats, quail, turkeys, a llama, ostriches and an assortment of other creatures. They were not afraid for themselves with a panther prowling the area but were concerned about their animals, which live outside in pens.

The Rays immediately called the county sheriff about the sighting, who referred them to animal control officers, who didn't believe their story. "People blow stories like this off," Mike Ray said, "but we've got something really big living out here." The couple went on to try and trap the beast, and even advertised for help on a local radio show, but the sightings eventually stopped. Whatever was out there in the woods eventually moved on.

In early 2004, a series of panther sightings plagued the isolated roads and stretches of woods in Calhoun County, a long and sparsely populated peninsula between the Mississippi and Illinois Rivers. The entire county has less than five thousand residents and is heavily timbered, with large bluffs, steep hills, and a large population of deer and wild turkey, food sources that cougars and panthers would thrive on. Some would say that if there really is a population of panthers living in Illinois—black panthers or otherwise—they would be hidden away in the vast forests of southern Illinois and in the wooded miles of Calhoun County.

In February 2004, two separate sightings of a black panther occurred in the small town of Hardin, Calhoun County's largest community, located along Illinois' Great River Road. In each case, witnesses described a pure black cat of extreme size. Experts speculated that perhaps the animal had escaped from captivity, but no animal parks, zoos, or private owners reported the loss of what would be a very expensive beast.

"If it is an escaped leopard or whatever, I am not sure what might bring them into town. I'm not familiar with large wild cats, though I have heard about panthers being in the county for almost ten years," Hardin police chief Jim Franke said about the two sightings that he had personally investigated. "If it is a cat that has escaped from captivity, it could depend upon people's garbage to survive, if it hasn't adequate hunting skills or has been declawed. But as far as cougars go, I have no doubt in my mind that they are here in Calhoun County and have been for years."

Derek Driesenga, of nearby Kampsville, the owner of Illinois Trophy Outfitters, operated a hunting lodge in Calhoun County and had long been aware that panthers roamed the dark woods around his property. He made many attempts over the years to produce evidence of their existence, including the documentation of tracks and attempts to photograph the animals. In October 2003, he was able to get one blurry photograph that does appear to show a large cat.

Chief Franke and Derek Driesenga are not alone in their belief that big cats roam the forests of the region. Alberta and Ted Dean of Dean's Market in Kampsville own a farm next to Driesenga's hunting property near Silver Creek. It is not far from where Driesenga photographed the cat. "I have heard about cougars or mountain lions, or some sort of big cat, roaming through Calhoun County for years but I simply never believed the stories until I saw Derek's picture," Alberta Dean said in an interview. "I've roamed the woods picking blackberries and hunting mushrooms all my life, but after seeing the picture, you couldn't get me to do that again."

Tom Rasp, from the O'Fallon area, became curious about the panther sightings around Hardin after reading some newspaper accounts of the reports. In May 2004, he decided to go and take a look for himself. Never expecting anything other than perhaps to talk to someone who had seen one of the big cats, he was driving down a back road one afternoon and was startled to have a panther sighting of his own. As he was riding his motorcycle slowly along unpaved Franklin Hill Road, about five miles south of Hardin, he suddenly came upon a large black cat walking down the middle of the roadway. As the cat turned and noticed him, it was startled and took off running into the woods.

Rasp couldn't believe what he had just seen but was careful to recall as many details about the encounter as he could. One thing that he did tell me was that he was sure that the cat had been black. After the cat ran off, Rasp immediately stopped his bike and followed the cat for a short distance, only stopping when he started to enter onto private property. He took a look around but didn't see the cat anywhere, so he decided to look for tracks instead. He soon realized that the cat had been crossing the road on what was apparently a game trail of some sort. As a lifelong hunter and outdoorsman, Tom recognized the way the grass had been pressed flat by passing animals. He searched in vain for any tracks.

"I know what I saw," he said. "It was a black panther. There was no doubt about that but where it came from, I don't know."

On March 11, 2010, a woman named Cyndie Simon, who was in Decatur for the funeral of her father, reported a large black panther near Lost Bridge Road on the city's east side.

She spotted the panther in a cul-de-sac in the Windsor Village area and it ducked between two houses just after 9:30 P.M. Four people saw the animal, first thinking it was a dog, before suddenly realizing that it was a huge cat. "What baffles me is how it just seemed to disappear into the dark," she said. "There were four of us who saw it. It was real."

Where do they come from? The theories about the comings and goings of black panthers are many, from wrecked circus trains to zoo escapes, but do these entertaining tales really explain the large numbers of sightings that have taken place all over the state? Many believe the panthers are simply "out of place" animals, which usually refers to creatures that are driven out of their normal habitats by the incursion of man, locations changing due to construction or highway work, or even devastation caused by nature in the form of storms, drought, or natural disasters. But just how far are we to believe these animals have wandered—across continents, rivers, or perhaps even oceans? This seems unlikely. Can the answer be a paranormal one? Are black panthers somehow "teleported" to Illinois by some unexplainable means? While this is the most bizarre theory, there are many who give it credence. And who can say? Is it any harder to believe than some of the more mundane theories that exist?

While it seems unlikely that escapes from circus trains, zoos, and private owners could create numbers high enough to explain all of the black panther sightings in Illinois, such an explanation just might shed light on some of the sightings in central Illinois in the 1960s and 1970s. My research into local black panthers led me to a woman named Kim Brown, who had grown up in Decatur along Christmas Tree Road, just off of Rea's Bridge Road. In the 1960s, this was still a rural and fairly secluded area east of town and, as noted earlier, was an area where a number of black panther sightings occurred.

Kim told me about a strange experience she and her family had while living on their farm, which was located just across the road from the old Shyer's Christmas Tree Farm. One night, the insistent barking of their German shepherd awakened everyone in the house. They went to see what was happening and in the illumination beneath a pole light in the yard was a huge cat. It was casually walking through the yard towards the barn. Kim described how the animal's tail "just seemed to float along behind it." They feared for the safety of the horses that they had in the barn, so they ran outside to try and scare the animal away.

As they ran out to the barnyard, they found their dog, frozen with fear and refusing to get close to the large cat, which stood watching them at the edge of the building. They got a good look at the creature and Kim recalled it being four or five feet long and weighing close to one hundred fifty pounds. "I could hear a slight purr coming from the cat, almost like a hum," she told me. Then the cat turned and strolled off into the darkness, vanishing into the cornfield.

A few days later, Kim and her mother spotted the cat again. This time, it was stretched out on the roof of their barn, enjoying the sun. They watched it for ten or fifteen minutes before it left. "We never figured out how it got up or down," she admitted. After that, they never saw the cat again, although they did sometimes hear it screaming in the forest at night. Kim remembered often finding its tracks along the creek behind the house. "I could never get my dog or pony to go along that creek with me," she told me.

Kim had no explanation for the tracks but her father often wondered if the animal might have cubs that it kept in one of the caves along the river. His theory was based on something unusual that he later told Kim about. Her father, who was an auxiliary deputy for the Macon County Sheriff's Department, told her that in the early or mid-1960s, a family across the road from Rea's Landing had an exotic animal "farm" in a cave by the river. Kim didn't know anything about it, but her father did. He said that the owners were supposed to have disposed of the animals but apparently they were unable to do so. The rumor was that they had set the animals loose instead. One of the animals was said to have been an adult panther. "Maybe that's where 'our' cat came from," Kim told me, "because he certainly didn't seem to be afraid of us."

The exotic animal farm, which was, needless to say, an illegal operation, was believed to have been closed down in 1967 or 1968. If there was a panther among the animals that were kept here, it just might explain the sightings that took place in Decatur in 1967, 1970, and perhaps even beyond. If the cub spotted on the Runyon farm was the offspring of this cat, perhaps generations of these same panthers are still lurking in the area today.

In recent years, after learning of the possible existence of the exotic animal farm, I have tried to track down further information about the farm or cave but so far, have found nothing. I have discovered a few people who also heard stories about the animals being released in the late 1960s but there is nothing in the official record, or newspaper accounts, about the farm.

The farm, like the panthers themselves, remains a mystery.

Nellie the Lion

As if black panthers were not strange enough, these anomalous beasts are not the only big cats to have mysteriously appeared in Illinois. There are scores of residents who accept the idea that black panthers often turn up within the state, but if these same people were asked to believe that an African lion once terrorized central Illinois, would they be so open-minded? According to newspaper and personal accounts from 1917, a lion did turn up near Monticello and for nearly a month, "Nellie the Lion" was the terror of the region.

The lion first appeared in July 1917 on the estate of Robert Allerton, located near Monticello. A lion of some sort had been reported on the grounds and had apparently killed several head of livestock. One afternoon, the Allerton butler, Thomas Gullett, was out picking flowers when he was attacked by what he referred to as an "African lioness." The butler suffered only minor cuts and scratches, but the search was soon on for the beast. I had the opportunity to speak with a relative of Mr. Gullett in 1990 and she told me that the attack was not only very real, but the most frightening event her relative had ever experienced. It was spoken of in the family for many years afterward and had since become a part of their lore.

Robert Allerton offered a $250 reward to the hunter that killed the animal, and soon, an armed posse of more than three hundred men turned up for a search of the large and heavily wooded estate. Allerton's farm manager bought a quantity of fresh meat and placed it in strategic locations. He hoped to lure the animal into a trap, but had no luck. The lion was seen later that day by two hunters who had given up on the search. Shortly after midnight, Paul and Lee Bear spotted the lion crossing a road in front of their truck. They managed to get off a few shots at it, but the lion jumped a fence and disappeared into a cornfield.

The search resumed the next day. While the hunters were tramping through the woods, the lion appeared again at the Allerton house. Mrs. Shaw, the chief housekeeper, got a good look at it, and like Gullett, described it as an "African lioness."

On July 17, tracks were discovered near Decatur and were reported as being five inches long and four inches wide. Two boys claimed to have seen the lion later that same day, prowling along the Sangamon River. They didn't see where the lion went since both of them took off running in the opposite direction.

Thanks to newspaper reports and wild rumors, public hysteria mounted in central Illinois. People mistook dogs for the lion and one farmer became involved a widely reported dispute about whether he had mistaken the headlights of an approaching vehicle for the beast's shining eyes. He denied it, but he couldn't explain why he had put a bullet into the truck's radiator!

What may have seemed funny in the newspapers came as no joke to Earl Hill, Chester Osborn, and the two men's wives on July 29. The two couples were motoring west of Decatur on the Springfield Road when the lion pounced on their car and tried to attack them. Hill and Osborn, sitting in the front seat of the vehicle, first saw the animal standing in the weeds on the side of the road. The animal jumped at them and collided with the vehicle, which was traveling at about twenty miles per hour. The couples hurriedly drove back to Decatur and summoned the police, who followed them back to the scene. To their surprise, the lion was still there, although it vanished over a hill when they arrived. The two lone policemen chose not to pursue it without heavier weapons. They returned in the early-morning hours with two carloads of other officers. The men were all armed with high-powered rifles. They searched the area for several hours; finding nothing, they returned to Decatur.

On July 31, a farmhand named James Rutherford spotted the lion near a gravel pit. The animal looked at him without interest and then wandered away. Rutherford gathered a group of hunters and brought them back to the scene. They found nothing but a number of paw prints and a half-eaten calf, which the owner stated had been missing for four days.

After that, Nellie vanished into oblivion and was never heard from again. Today, the story is only remembered as a legend, but newspapers and testimony of the era assure us that the lion really did exist.

Illinois's Phantom Kangaroos

What could be even stranger than big cats? Believe it or not, reports of mysterious kangaroos have been surprisingly widespread in Illinois, despite the fact that these animals are literally thousands of miles from their native habitat. Are the kangaroos, like the Illinois black panthers, refugees from zoos or wrecked circus trains, or some sort of mystery beasts that come and go without explanation? Strangely, there are sketchy records of kangaroos, or "hopping monkeys" in the Midwest that date back many years. However, it would not be until the middle 1970s that "kangaroo mania" would sweep across Illinois.

The event that started the Illinois kangaroo flap occurred in the early-morning hours of October 18, 1974, when two Chicago police officers answered a call from a resident on the northwest side of the city. The caller claimed that a kangaroo was sitting on his front porch, peering into the window.

Not surprisingly, the peculiar call was received with a good laugh from radio dispatchers, but it didn't seem so funny a few hours later when the two officers who investigated the report had the five-foot-high animal cornered in a dark alley. Patrolmen Leonard Ciagi and Michael Byrne approached the growling animal with caution and inexplicably thought that it would be a good idea to try and put handcuffs on it. Byrne gave this a try and the kangaroo suddenly started screeching and became vicious. It began punching the officers in the face and kicking them in the shins. Understandably, the officers backed away; short of using their guns, they found that they had no way to subdue or capture the animal. A minute or two later, additional squad cars arrived and the kangaroo took off at high speed. It cleared a fence and vanished into the darkness, leaving some puzzled officers with sore shins behind.

The incident made the newspapers and became the first in a rash of sightings. Reports began to flood in from all over the

Chicago area. The kangaroos were just arriving in Illinois, or more likely, people were just starting to talk about what they were seeing. On the same afternoon as the officers' early-morning encounter, a four-and-a-half-foot-tall kangaroo was reported hopping down the street in Oak Park. The next afternoon, October 19, a young man who was delivering newspapers heard the screech of car brakes behind him. He turned to look and saw a kangaroo hopping across the intersection of Sunnyside and Mulligan Streets. "He looked at me, I looked at him, and away he hopped," Kenneth Grieshamer later recalled.

About an hour later, the kangaroo was reported again near Austin and Eastwood Roads and later that evening, an anonymous call to the Chicago Police Department pinpointed the mysterious animal around Belmont and Mango Avenues. The following morning, police dispatchers fielded a number of calls from concerned residents who had seen the kangaroo rummaging through their garbage cans.

Two days later, another young man spotted a kangaroo while waiting for the school bus. As he stood on the corner just off of Irving Park Road on the city's North Side, he caught a bit of motion to his left and turned quickly to see the animal as it crossed the street and disappeared into a neighboring yard.

On October 23, a kangaroo was seen roaming through Schiller Woods, near Irving Park Road. This was the last sighting until November. For a short time, things stayed quiet in Chicago.

The next sighting occurred on November 1 in Plano. John Orr, an off-duty police officer, spotted the kangaroo on Riverview Road, just outside of town. The animal jumped about eight feet from the edge of a cornfield and landed in the middle of the road, directly in the headlights of Orr's car. "I'm positive that I saw him," Orr stated. "People don't believe you when you see things like that but I definitely know that it was a kangaroo. If I hadn't slowed down, I would have hit him.

My cousin was in the car behind me and when she saw him, she just plain ran off the road." After pausing for a moment in front of the vehicles, the kangaroo hopped off into a wooded area and disappeared.

The next night, November 2, three young men—Jerry Wagner, Steve Morton and Shawnee Clark—were driving along Shafer Road in Plano when their headlights illuminated something in the middle of the road. As they swerved to the side, all of them got a good look at it and realized that it was a full-grown kangaroo. The startled animal hopped over a five-foot fence and took off into the woods.

The three men reported the sighting to the Kendall County Sheriff's Office. At the same time as that sighting, a similar incident was taking place with the same—or an identical—kangaroo about fifty miles away in Chicago.

A young couple named Cathy Battaglia and Len Zeglicz were out for a walk around 9:30 that evening and spotted a strange creature hunched on the side of South New England Avenue. At first they thought that it was a dog but when the animal turned and looked at them, and then raised up and hopped away, they realized they were looking at a kangaroo. Since it seems unlikely that a kangaroo could travel more than fifty miles in only a few minutes, one has to wonder just how many kangaroos were hopping around Illinois in November 1974.

On the morning of November 3, the kangaroo, or one of them anyway, was spotted by a Frank Kocherver near a forest preserve on Chicago's Northwest side.

The next day, November 4, a truck driver saw a deer and what he thought was a kangaroo near Plano. The driver pulled his rig over to the side of the road and followed the animal tracks into the woods. He easily recognized the trail left by the deer but the other animal was "definitely not a deer." The driver was sure the strange tracks had belonged to a kangaroo.

The last Illinois sighting in 1974 occurred near Lansing when a truck driver was forced to swerve off the highway to avoid hitting one of the errant creatures. After a few more sightings in Indiana, kangaroos disappeared off the radar until the following year, when they came back to Illinois once again.

On July 14, 1975, Rosemary Hopwood was traveling along Route 128 near Dalton City and was surprised to see an animal on the side of the road that she at first mistook for a dog. She looked again and realized that the tan-colored animal was a kangaroo. It hopped away into a cornfield and disappeared. Three days later, several other people also reported seeing a kangaroo in the general area.

Later that month, another kangaroo sighting occurred near DuQuoin. Kevin Luthi was one of several people who saw a five-foot high kangaroo hopping along side roads and into cornfields near the small southern Illinois community.

The next reports came the following year, in April 1976, and took place near Rock Island. Local resident Harry Masterson spotted a kangaroo near his home on April 6. He was out walking his dog around six-thirty in the morning when he saw it. "I looked across the street and there it was," he said. "It was a kangaroo and a big one. It came hopping across the yard. The kangaroo and I stood there looking at each other for a minute. Then it turned and hopped away to the north."

As the animal began to spring away down the street, Masterson ran into the house and talked his wife, Barbara, into coming outside and taking a look. By the time she ran out into the yard, the creature was already on its way. Barbara later commented that it moved "faster than a dog." Barbara's mother came out and joined them, and all of them watched as the kangaroo vanished down the street.

After that, the kangaroo flap of the 1970s came to an end. This doesn't mean that the mysterious creatures have disappeared from Illinois for good. No one ever knew where the kangaroos came from, where they went to, or when they might be back.

Illinois Water Creatures

One of the most famous urban legends of all time claimed that alligators lived in the sewers of some of our major American cities. The stories alleged that these reptiles had been brought back from Florida shortly after hatching. Once the alligators started to grow, concerned parents realized that their children's pets would soon turn into creatures of monstrous proportions. They quickly flushed them down the toilet. Once in the sewer system, the alligators grew to be huge, feeding off the rats and the garbage of the city and occasionally eating the unsuspecting utility worker or unlucky homeless person.

The story seems too wild to be true, but the reader might be surprised to learn that it actually has a basis in fact. Newspapers and books have featured a number of accounts from sewer workers who have encountered these beasts over the years. Anything might be possible under the streets of New York, but what about the streets of Illinois? It may be hard to imagine that alligators can make appearances in the waters of the Prairie State, far away from their natural habitat, but records and reports show that they have turned up here on occasion.

One of the first reports of an erratic alligator dates back to 1902, when a two-and-a-half-foot long creature was seen swimming in the South Branch of the Chicago River, near the Twelfth Street Bridge. Police officer Daniel McCarthy and bridge ironworker James Burke first spotted the creature. After watching it swim about for a few minutes, McCarthy drew his revolver and fired four times at the gator, but failed to hit it. Burke then made a noose out of a heavy piece of twine and leaned out over the water to try and snag it. Instead of capturing the alligator, he fell into the river. After some difficulty getting out of the water, he renewed his efforts and finally managed to snag the gator. The two men took it to a nearby shack and it was later placed in a barrel of water so that neighborhood children could take a look at it. What became of the alligator in unknown.

In 1937, another gator was spotted in a creek leading into Lake Decatur in central Illinois. In October 1966, two fishermen captured a small alligator that measured a little over a foot long on this same lake. The two men were fishing when they discovered the baby alligator in the company of its much larger mother. They estimated the parent creature to be around six feet long. At the sight of the larger alligator, they abandoned their fishing spot, taking the smaller animal with them. The local newspaper featured a story on the two fishermen that contained a photograph of one of the men, Richard Stubblefield, holding the baby alligator.

In June 1967, Decatur's sewer system disgorged an alligator of its own when a creature was pulled from a drainpipe at 895 West Eldorado Street. The animal was less than a foot long, but it must have had a mother somewhere. Was she also lurking nearby?

Three years later, in June 1970, an alligator was pulled from the waters of a manmade lake near Lombard. Animal control officers who investigated the discovery, which had been made by a group of local children swimming in the lake, speculated that the animal had been released from captivity when it had overgrown its tank.

Another alligator was spotted in the Sangamon River near Oakley in August 1971. One year later, in August 1972, another alligator was spotted strolling across Route 66 near Chenoa. This one stopped traffic along the highway for a few minutes before it was taken away by befuddled police officers.

In June 2008, a forty-five-pound alligator was discovered swimming in the Chicago River. The creature was spotted again on the South Side in an area that was known in the early 1900s as "Bubbly Creek" because of the waste that was dumped into it by the local slaughterhouses. The gator was captured by volunteers from the Chicago Herpetological Society and shipped to a reptile sanctuary in the southeastern United States, which is where the beast actually belonged.

Alligators, obviously, should not be found in Chicago, which is why everyone was so surprised when another one showed up in the river on August 6, 2010. The two-and-a-half-foot creature was quickly captured by "Alligator Bob," a reptile expert from the Chicago Herpetological Society who is known only by his first name. Just three weeks later, on August 24, Bob was called out again when another gator turned up. The three-foot creature was spotted in the murky waters under the Belmont Avenue Bridge. Bob managed to snag this one, too. No one knows where the creatures came from, although Bob surmised that they may have been someone's pets.

Are there more alligators lurking in the darkness under Chicago, and perhaps beneath other cities and small towns in Illinois? If baby alligators are being pulled from the river, is there a chance that there are a few fully grown versions of these creatures out there?

That's definitely something to think about the next time you pass an open storm drain!

Out-of-place alligators are strange, but there are even weirder things in the waters of Illinois' lakes and ponds.

At one point in the 1800s, Lake Michigan claimed to have a mystery inhabitant to rival the monsters of Lake Champlain and various other bodies of water where long-necked beasts were believed to dwell. An August 1867 edition of the *Chicago Tribune* asserted that hundreds of witnesses observed some type of "lake monster" from both shore and water during several days of the summer. A newspaper writer added, "that Lake Michigan is inhabited by a vast monster, part fish and part serpent, no longer admits of doubt."

The newspaper reported that the crews of the tugboat *George S. Wood* and the propeller boat *Skylark* spotted the creature moving through the water just off the Evanston shoreline. The crews reported that the monster was between forty and fifty feet long and had a neck as thick as that of a person and a body that was as big around as a barrel. A few days later, on August 6, a fisherman named Joseph Muhike encountered the same, or a nearly identical, beast about a mile and a half from the Hyde Park section of Chicago.

The creature was seen off and on over the course of the next decade, but the sightings eventually dropped off and nothing has been heard from the "Lake Michigan Monster" in many years.

When I was growing up, my parents had a small pond at the edge of some fields and woods about a mile or so from our house. My brother and I spent many summer hours fishing in the pond, mostly for small catfish. The fish were always plentiful; as fast as you could bait a hook and toss it into the water, you could count on something at the other end of the line. Then, one summer in the early 1980s, the pond changed. The fish stopped biting and it was almost as if they had disappeared. We pondered this for several days and then saw something moving in the water. As we watched the water rippling at the deepest point in the center of the pond, we were startled to suddenly see a large head appear above the surface. We only got a glimpse of it that time, but it was big, oddly shaped, and ugly. It quickly disappeared back under the water and even though we continued watching, we saw nothing else strange that day.

Over the next couple of weeks we came to the pond almost every afternoon. On just about every occasion, we saw something very large moving in the water. We had no idea what it could be but imagined the worst. We feared that a huge snake or a water monster of some sort had taken up residence in the pond. The creature's size was likely wreaking havoc on the wildlife in the pond, which would explain the disappearance of the fish that we had been catching before its arrival. Eventually, the creature moved on, following a drought later in the summer that dropped the water level in the pond to a pretty extreme level.

Looking back now, I realize that the mysterious monster was likely nothing more than a large snapping turtle that ate up the small fish and preferred to remain in the darkness of the deepest part of the pond. However, I'll never forget the chills that we used to get whenever we saw it moving near the surface and how we were unable to figure out just what was moving through the cool depths. The pond would ripple and break, sending small waves out across the glassy surface as something came to the top and then plunged back down again. I'm sure it was a turtle, but what if it wasn't? What if the creature that lurked in the pond was something even stranger than what swam through our imaginations?

In the summer of 1879, residents of DuQuoin began experiencing their own weird sightings around what is called the Stump Pond. But whatever was living in their pond was certainly not a snapping turtle!

The Stump Pond was a fishing lake that had been left behind by strip mining, located on the Hayes Fair Acres Estate near town. It was close to the site of the harness track that would later host the famed Hambletonian race and was a place that was widely known in the region. This may have been what made the pond seem, to most people, like such an unlikely place to find a monster.

The mysterious creature was first encountered one evening in the summer of 1879. A local man named Paquette was fishing on the lake one night when, he said, something rushed through the water beneath him with enough force to rock his boat. Frightened, he immediately returned to shore and vowed that he would never venture out away from the banks again after dark. The following summer, in 1880, two local miners claimed that they saw a twelve-foot-long "serpent" in the water. They said that it was dark green and had a body that was as thick as a telegraph pole. The monster put in a brief appearance and then vanished back into the depths. The miners, meanwhile, decided that they were no longer in the mood for fishing.

Reports continued to come from Stump Pond for many years. In 1965, Allyn Dunmyer, a retired miner, was in his boat on the shallow waters of the pond when something startled the creature. He believed that the monster was hiding in the muddy area near the shore but some sort of noise caused it to stir. It passed directly under his boat as it headed for deeper water and as it did, the serpent hit the boat with its head. "It liked to have turned the boat clear over," Dunmyer said. Dunmyer had seen a monster—or monsters—in the pond before. "I think there is more than one of the critters in the pond," he said. "I've seen them so near the surface that their back fins were sticking out of the water."

Another man, who was wading in the pond, said that he stumbled upon something sleeping under the algae that covered the water. As it sped away from him, he stated that he thought the creature looked like a large alligator. Herb Heath, a DuQuoin businessman who also saw the creature, claimed that the monster was "as big as I am, maybe bigger."

The stories of the "Stump Pond Monster" continued until 1968, when the water was partially drained from the lake and the fish cleared out of it with electric stunners. What the locals found there in the muddy remains of the pond led some to believe the monster was nothing more than an overgrown catfish. A number of the fish weighed in at more than thirty pounds, which is awfully big for a catfish, but is that big enough for one of them to have been mistaken for the creature that had been dubbed a monster?

The Legend of the Piasa Bird

Travelers along the Great River Road near the small town of Alton are often surprised to see a rock painting on the side of a bluff that portrays a pretty vicious-looking winged creature. Years ago, this painting was actually a petroglyph that showed two such creatures. These monsters were called the "Piasa" by the Illiniwek Indians. The original painting existed near this location for hundreds of years and was first described in the journals of Pere Marquette, written while he was exploring the Mississippi River in 1673. The original site of the painting is now long gone, but Marquette described the creatures portrayed there in this manner:

> While skirting some rocks, which by their height and length inspired awe, we saw upon one of them two painted monsters which at first made us afraid, and upon which the boldest savages dare not long rest their eyes. They are as large as a calf; they have horns on their heads like those of a deer, a horrible look, red eyes, a beard like a tiger's, a face somewhat like a man's, a

body covered with scales, and so long a tail that winds all around the body, passing above the head and going back between the legs, ending in a fish's tail. Green, red and black are the colors composing the picture. Moreover, these two monsters are so well painted that we cannot believe any savage is their author; for good painters in France would find it difficult to reach that place conveniently to paint them.

Marquette also added a drawing of the creatures to his journal account, but the drawing was unfortunately lost a short time later when his canoe capsized. In 1678, though, a map drawn by French mapmaker Jean-Baptiste Louis Franquelin included a picture of the fierce Piasa, based on Marquette's writings.

Father Louis Hennepin, another early explorer of the West, published a book in 1698 called *A New Discovery of a Vast Country in America* and he also wrote about seeing the paintings of the Piasa, which were first cut into the bluff and then painted over. Unlike Father Marquette, Hennepin included in his the description that the Piasa had wings, making it a fearsome bird rather than simply an Indian monster. The reason for this was discovered many years later.

In 1812, the first use of the word "Piasa" appeared in print. Major Amos Stoddard, who had been earlier appointed by President Thomas Jefferson as commander of the northern portion of the Louisiana Purchase, wrote "What they call 'painted monsters' on the side of a high perpendicular rock, apparently inaccessible to man, located between the Missouri and Illinois Rivers and known to moderns by the name of Piasa, still remains to a good degree of preservation."

In 1820, Captain Gideon Spencer came up the Mississippi and got a glimpse of the Piasa. By this time, though, only one of the paintings remained. The fate of the second creature is unknown but it's likely that it was destroyed by weather and falling rock, as the bluffs near Alton can be dangerously unstable at times. Spencer asked the Indians what the strange painting was and they told him that it was a "Storm Bird" or a "Thunder Bird" and that it had been placed there long ago. The Indians would fire their guns at it and some would offer it tobacco by lighting their pipes and blowing smoke in the direction of the image.

The Piasa painting was located immediately below the site of the first Illinois state penitentiary in Alton. The painting was partially destroyed in the 1840s when quarrying was done on the bluff by convicts from the prison. Additional work done in the 1860s, when the abandoned prison was used as a Confederate prisoner of war camp, ruined what was left of it.

The painting was later described by Professor William McAdams, an Illinois State Geologist who created an illustration of the bird in the 1880s. It is from his drawing that all of the modern-day renditions of the Piasa Bird come. McAdams also seems to be the person responsible for creating the mythology of a single bird-like creature, instead of two monsters, as the Indians originally told the story. In McAdams's day, the original painting no longer existed. A quarry had purchased the property and, using convict labor, blasted away the wall and the petroglyph around 1847. The drawing that McAdams created was based on the testimony of five men who recalled seeing the painting before it was destroyed. It was later featured in the *Literary Digest* and it is believed to be the most accurate drawing of the Piasa.

Some critics of McAdams have claimed that he created the mythology of the Piasa as a bird instead of simply a Native American monster. The evidence they cite is that the Piasa had never been written about or drawn with wings prior to McAdams's version in *Literary Digest*, but this is not the case. Another similar painting that was done of the Piasa at roughly this same time was created by a man named Ladd, a former mayor of White Hall, Illinois. According to Ladd, he based his picture on a recollection of the original image that had been given to him by "Spencer Russell of Bluffdale, who had been nearer to the Piasa than any person now living." He spoke to the man, who told him this:

I used to climb the rocks to look at it when I was a boy. I have been within sixty feet of it. I once pointed it out from the deck of an English steamer to a lady and she looked at it through a field glass. No wings showed that day for the weather was dry. The colors were always affected by dampness, and it stood out distinctly after rain. Father Marquette evidently saw the Piasa on a dry day for he pictured it without wings.

Some have also claimed that the word "Piasa" was never a part of the language of the Illinois Indians, but this does not seem to be the case either. In 1883, the Bureau of Ethnology described the word as an Illinois Indian name denoting "a bird that devours men." Even among the Sauk Indians, relatives of the Illinois, the name was known and the famous Black Hawk's father was himself called Pyesa.

Who created the original painting? No one will ever know for sure, but it must have existed for some time as part of the culture of the local Native Americans. It was said that on a flat ledge below the painting were hundreds of arrowheads and spear points. It is believed that the Indians who passed the Piasa on the river would "attack" the creature by firing an arrow at it. It apparently became a custom when floating past the future site of Alton. The Piasa Bird is considered one of the most enduring legends of the region—a tall tale, an Indian myth that is sufficient to entertain children. But what if it isn't? What if there is more to the "legend" than meets the eye?

The legend of the Piasa Bird dates back to long before Europeans came to region. It has been traced to a band of

Illiniwek Indians who lived along the Mississippi in the area north of present-day Alton. This tribe, led by a chief named Owatoga, hunted and fished the valley and the river and lived a contented life until the "great beast" came.

One morning, Owatoga's son, Utim, and a friend were fishing when they heard a terrible scream. They looked and saw a huge bird rising from the edge of the river. The legend states that the bird was of such dimensions that it could carry away a full-grown deer in its talons, and that once it obtained a taste for human flesh, it would eat nothing else. The creature the two men saw had a young man gripped in its claws and it carried him away and out of sight. Quickly, the two young men returned to their village and found their people very frightened. They waited all day for the young man to escape from the bird and return, but he did not.

After that, nearly every morning, the great bird would appear in the sky and carry away a member of the tribe, be it man, woman, or child. Those who were carried off were never seen again. The people began to call the bird the "Piasa," which meant "the bird which devours men." Owatoga realized that they were powerless against this beast and he retreated to his lodge to fast and to pray for guidance. He emerged the next day with a plan that had been revealed to him in a vision.

According to his vision, Owatoga was to take six of his finest braves and climb to the top of one of the highest bluffs. The young men were to carry with them only their bows and a quiver of poisoned arrows. They were to hide themselves while Owatoga stood on the edge of the bluff and waited for the Piasa to appear. When the monster came, the chief was to throw himself down on the rocks and hold on while the bird attempted to carry him away. As it did so, the braves would appear with their bows and slay the beast.

Of course, all of the men in the tribe offered to help kill the Piasa, but Owatoga chose only young, unmarried men, his own son among them. The arrows were sharpened and poisoned and the group climbed to the top of the bluff. The six young men hid themselves beneath a rock ledge and Owatoga stepped out to the edge of the cliff. He folded his arms and waited for the creature to appear. Suddenly, the sky darkened overhead and the bird's massive wings were heard. The Piasa swooped down toward Owatoga. Just as the tip of the creature's sharp talon sunk into his shoulder, Owatoga threw himself flat upon the rocks. His hands curled around the roots of a tree and he clung desperately to them. The Piasa roared in frustration and its wings beat furiously, trying to lift the Indian from the rocks.

The wings unfolded once more, and as the bird exposed its body, the young men burst from their hiding place and fired their arrows at the beast. The arrows found their mark but the Piasa continued to fight, trying again and again to lift Owatoga from the rocks. Then, with a howl of agony, the creature released him and collapsed backward, crashing over the edge of the bluff. It spiraled down out of sight and plunged beneath the waters of the Mississippi. The terrible creature was never seen again.

Despite his wounds, Owatoga recovered from the battle and joined in the celebration over the death of the Piasa. The tribe ate, danced, and celebrated into the night and the next day, and they painted a colorful tribute to the Piasa bird on the stone face of the bluff where it had been destroyed. From that time on, any Indian who went up or down the river fired an arrow at the image of the Piasa Bird in memory of their deliverance from the monster.

When Europeans settled this region and heard the tales of the Piasa, they found no evidence (at first) to suggest that this creature really existed. But the Indians who still lived here at that time certainly believed it had. As mentioned previously, they took great pleasure in loosing arrows at the creature as they passed on the river; later generations would fire their rifles at it.

In July 1836, John Russell discovered something very unusual concerning the legend of the Piasa Bird. Russell was a professor at Shurtleff College in Alton and had interest enough in the local legend to do a little exploring and research into the story of the creature. His adventures were later recounted in an 1848 magazine article and in *Records of Ancient Races in the Mississippi Valley* by William McAdams in 1887. Here is how his story appears, written in his own words:

Near the close of March of the present year, I was induced to visit the bluffs below the mouth of the Illinois River, above that of the Piasa. My curiosity was principally directed to the examination of a cave, connected with the above tradition as one of those to which the bird had carried his human victims.

Preceded by an intelligent guide, who carried a spade, I set out on my excursion. The cave was extremely difficult of access, and at one point in our progress I stood at an elevation of one hundred fifty feet on the perpendicular face of the bluff, with barely room to sustain one foot. The unbroken wall towered above me, while below me was the river.

After a long and perilous climb, we reached the cave, which was about fifty feet above the surface of the river. . . . The roof of the cavern was vaulted, and the top was hardly less than twenty feet high. The shape of the cavern was irregular; but, so far as I could judge, the bottom would average twenty by thirty feet.

The floor of the cavern throughout its whole extent was one mass of human bones. Skulls and other bones were mingled in the utmost confusion. To what depth they extended I was unable to decide; but we dug to a depth of 3 or 4 feet in every part of the cavern, and still we found only bones. The remains of thousands must have been deposited here. How, and by whom, and for what purpose, it is impossible to conjecture.

In 1873, Martin Beem authored an article on the Piasa Legend for the *Illinois State Journal* of Springfield. The legend he tells of is similar to that recounted by Professor Russell, and he also described the Indian bones that were found in the cave. With the publication of these articles, the story grew and was told and retold countless times. In 1875, author A. D. Jones wrote about the paintings, and not long after, Edmund Flagg, on a tour of the western country, claimed that he also saw the bone-filled cave and corroborated Russell's story.

Was this cave really the lair of the Piasa Bird? Did this bird, always thought to be merely a mythological creature, actually exist? Did the monster really carry off and slay a large number of Native Americans who once lived in this region?

As a simple answer to a number of complex questions—no one really knows. The mystery of the Piasa Bird remains unsolved, and while many have gone in search of this elusive cave over the years, none have yet been able to find it. This is not as strange as the reader might think, though. There are many remote areas in this immediate region, overgrown by forests, lost among the bluffs, and simply forgotten. Homes, buildings, churches, and cemeteries have all just been left to the elements and so it's very possible that the same thing could happen with natural formations like caves, hundreds of which are scattered through the bluffs along the river. What may be the legendary cave of the Piasa Bird remains elusive today, as do the true origins of the story.

Was the bird real? It's certainly possible, for the Piasa Bird was not the only mysterious flying creature that has terrorized the residents of Illinois.

Thunderbirds Over Illinois

There are perhaps no accounts in the annals of the mysterious in Illinois that are as strange as those of giant birds that swoop across the sky, frightening the unsuspecting and then vanishing back into the clouds. Illinois has an inordinate number of such sightings and encounters, including the legendary Piasa Bird and the famous "Lawndale Thunderbird Attack." Such accounts are certainly the reason that many Illinoisans keep watching the sky as they travel the highways, woods, and fields of the state.

American Indian lore is filled with stories of strange, monstrous birds with enormous wingspans and the propensity to carry away human victims. They called these creatures "Thunderbirds" because the legends claimed that their flapping wings made a sound like rolling thunder. The birds have been described as having wingspans of twenty feet or more, hooked talons, and razor-sharp beaks; the descriptions, like that of Alton's Piasa Bird, at times seem oddly close to the pterodactyls or other ancient flying creatures of prehistoric times.

But not all of the accounts of these winged creatures come from centuries ago. Many of them are more recent than most of us would like and occur uncomfortably close to home.

One of the earliest reports of an attack by a giant bird was documented in Tippah County, Missouri, in 1868. According to the report, an eight-year-old child was actually carried off by what was described by his teacher as an "eagle." It happened one day during school. The teacher's account states that "a sad tragedy occurred at my school a few days ago." He wrote that eagles had been very troublesome in the neighborhood, carrying off small pigs and lambs. No one thought that they would ever bother the local children until one afternoon when one of the birds swept down and picked up a boy named Jemmie Kenney and flew off with him. The other children called out but by the time the teacher ran outside to see what was going on, he could only hear the child screaming as he vanished into the sky. The teacher and the children on the playground began to cry out to raise the alarm in town and apparently, the noise frightened the bird and it dropped the boy. "But his talons had been buried in him so deeply, and the fall was so great, that he was killed," the teacher wrote.

What could this creature have really been? Could it have actually been an eagle? If so, it must have been a monstrous one. According to renowned zoologist Dr. Bernard Heuvelmans, even the most powerful eagle cannot lift more than a rabbit or a lamb. Most experts insist that even the strongest birds cannot carry off a small child, but this statement would be disproven by an event that occurred in Illinois in 1977.

But the accounts from the 1970s were not the first modern-day encounters with giant birds in Illinois. That first rash of sightings began in January 1948. One afternoon, a twelve-year-old boy named James Trares was playing outside of his parents' home in Glendale when he saw something that sent him running into the house to find his mother. "There's a bird outside as big as a B-29!" he shouted. He knew that what he had spotted was not a plane because he had seen it flapping its wings. The creature, which was grayish in color, was flying toward the sun. The Trares family did not discuss the sighting with anyone until a few months later, when news of giant birds began spreading across the state.

The newspapers widely reported the stories. On April 4, a former Army colonel named Walter F. Siegmund revealed that he had seen a gigantic bird in the sky above Alton. He had been talking with a local farmer and Colonel Ralph Jackson, the head of the Western Military Academy, at the time. "I thought there was something wrong with my eyesight," he said, "but it was definitely a bird and not a glider or a jet plane. It appeared to be flying northeast . . . from the movements of the object and its size, I figured it could only be a bird of tremendous size."

A few days later, a farmer from Caledonia named Robert Price would see the same, or a similar, bird. He called it a "monster bird . . . bigger than an airplane." A short time later, a truck driver from Freeport, Veryl Babb, came forward with corroborating testimony about the bird that Price had seen. He didn't report it initially because he feared that people would laugh at him. "When I read that Price had seen it I decided to report all about it," he said.

On April 10, another sighting took place, this time in Overland. Mr. and Mrs. Clyde Smith and Les Bacon spotted a huge bird from the Smiths' backyard, just before noon. They said they thought the creature was an airplane until it started to flap its wings furiously. The bird appeared to be dark gray in color and very large. "I thought it was a type of plane I had never seen before," Clyde Smith told reporters. "It was circling and banking in a way I had never seen a plane perform, and I kept waiting for it to fall."

On April 24, the bird was back in Alton. It was sighted by E. M. Coleman and his son, James. "It was an enormous, incredible thing with a body that looked like a naval torpedo," Coleman recalled later. "It was flying at about five hundred feet and cast a shadow the same size as a Piper Cub at that height."

The bird then apparently crossed the Mississippi River into St. Louis, where it was seen by patrolmen Clarence Johnson and Francis Hennelly of the St. Louis Police Department. "The thing was as big as a small airplane. Its wings were flapping, and it was headed southwest, flying at an altitude of several hundred feet. I thought it was a large eagle, but I've never seen one that big before," Johnson said.

Two days later, the bird was spotted by a St. Louis chiropractor, Dr. Kristine Dolezal, and on May 3, it was seen by instructors at the Mississippi School of Aeronautics at Lambert Airfield (now Lambert-St. Louis International Airport). They said that the "awfully big bird" was flying at an altitude of about twelve hundred feet. Less than twenty-four hours later, the bird was reported near Kings Highway by salesman Harry Bradford. He stopped his car and put his spotlight on it. The bird circled for a moment or two and then streaked away to the north.

By this time, letters were flooding into the office of Alton mayor Aloys P. Kaufmann. People were demanding to know why nothing was being done about the bird. "Perhaps it's a man-killing bird," one letter suggested. Many offered to try and shoot down the beast and others offered theories: it was a blue heron, an albatross, or a pelican—all of which were unlikely considering the size and behavior of the bird. The mayor, hoping to avoid dealing with the situation at all, passed things off to his assistant, Charles Hertenstein, who was given instructions to try and trap the creature. Luckily, he never had to attempt it.

On May 5, the bird was sighted for the last time in Alton. A man named Arthur Davidson called the police that evening to report the bird flying above the city.

Shortly after, the bird vanished from the Illinois skies. Ironically, just when the public excitement over the bird reached its peak, the sightings came to an end.

The Lawndale Thunderbird Attack

One of the most exciting and frightening Illinois encounters with giant birds occurred in 1977 in Lawndale, a small town in Logan County. On the evening of July 25, two giant birds appeared in the sky above the town. It was a warm, humid evening and three boys were playing hide-and-seek in the backyard of Ruth and Jake Lowe. The boys—Travis Goodwin, Michael Thompson, and Marlon Lowe—were in the yard at about 8:30 P.M. when the two birds approached the area from the south. Marlon Lowe later told newspapers that the boys first saw the birds swoop toward Travis Goodwin, who ran from the birds and jumped into a small, plastic swimming pool that was in the yard. The birds then swerved and headed toward Marlon. One of the birds grasped the boy's sleeveless shirt, snagging its talons in the cloth. The boy tried in vain to fight the bird off, crying loudly for help.

Marlon's cries were heard by Ruth and Jake Lowe, as well as by their friends Betty and Jim Daniels, who had been helping clean out a camper in the Lowes' driveway. They came running to see what was going on. As Marlon screamed for his mother, Mrs. Lowe appeared in time to see the bird actually lift the boy from the ground and into the air. The bird might not have released Marlon if he had not hammered at it with his fists. The bird had carried him, at a height of about three feet, across the yard for a distance of about thirty-five feet. Ruth was sure that if she had not come outside and startled the bird, it would have been able to carry the boy away. She later stated that the bird had been bending down, trying to peck at the boy as it carried him off. Luckily, although scratched and badly frightened, Marlon was not seriously injured.

Ruth Lowe later stated: "The birds just cleared the top of the camper, went beneath some telephone wires and flapped their wings, very gracefully, one more time."

The other three adults appeared on the scene within seconds of the attack. They said the birds were black, with bands of white around their necks. They had long, curved beaks and a wingspan of at least ten feet. The two birds were last seen flying toward some trees near Kickapoo Creek.

Following his release from the bird's talons, Marlon ran inside the camper that was parked in the driveway and refused to come out for a long time. He had not been badly injured by the experience but his shirt was tattered and torn. His mother reported afterward that he was unable to sleep the night after the incident—or for many nights to come. "He kept fighting those birds all night long," she said.

On the evening of the attack, Mrs. Lowe called the police and a game warden to report what had occurred. She said that she decided to call them because of her concern for other children who lived nearby, especially those who swam and fished in Kickapoo Creek, which was located in the direction the birds were flying in after the attack. Deputies from the Logan County Sheriff's Department searched the area around the creek on July 25 and 26 but found no evidence of the birds.

Investigator Jerry Coleman, who lived in Decatur at the time, was able to interview the Lowe family and the other witnesses within hours of the incident and wrote a detailed account of the event. He returned to Lawndale two years later to speak to the family again and discovered that they had been harassed and bothered by media attention and by others in the community. It was not uncommon for them to find dead birds on their doorstep in the morning, placed there by mean-spirited pranksters.

Marlon Lowe also had trouble dealing with the frightening encounter. The shock of the incident took years to wear off. Ruth Lowe had vivid memories of the event and spent years trying to identify the huge winged creatures that had almost taken her son. She spent long hours looking through books, certain that the creature had not been a turkey vulture, as an area game warden tried to convince her it was. "I was standing at the door," she told the investigators, "and all I saw was Marlon's feet dangling in the air. There aren't any birds around here that can lift him up like that."

After hours and hours spent looking at photographs and illustrations of large birds, Ruth Lowe decided that the closest thing that she could find to the birds that attacked her son were California condors. Marlon Lowe agreed that these birds were the most similar to what they had seen. Michael Thompson, one of the other boys that had been in the yard that day, agreed that the birds had been, or at least had looked like, condors.

Interestingly, though, California condors are nearly extinct creatures that, until 1987, could only be found in the wild living in the deserts of southern California. Their coloring does not match the birds reported in Lawndale, nor does their size, and they are not capable of picking up a small child. Out of all of the known birds, however, they looked most like the Illinois Thunderbirds. The question still lingers though: What if the mysterious creatures were not a "known bird"?

This was just one of the many problems that caused the negative public reaction toward the Lowes. Because the reports were so strange—and seemingly could not have happened— local wildlife officials immediately denied that the attack could have taken place. Logan County conservation officer A. A. Mervar was quoted as saying that "I don't think the child was picked up." Vern Wright, a biologist with the Illinois Department of Conservation in Springfield, told the press that the flying creature definitely did not pick up the boy. Many Illinois newspapers were not kind either. One Chicago paper ran a headline that read: "Expert: 'Attack' Tale is for the Birds." The first paragraph of the article consisted of only two words: "Thoroughly Ridiculous!"

But not all of the media outlets, or the general public, were so skeptical. Many newspapers picked up the story in the days following the attack and continued to update readers over the next few months as the birds (or very similar ones) continued their journey across Illinois. Ruth Lowe was interviewed by dozens of newspapers and received scores of telephone calls that promised support. "Some people did call to say that they believed me," Ruth Lowe later remembered.

The Lawndale Attack of July 1977 was just the start of the Thunderbird sightings in Illinois.

The ridicule that the Lowes suffered following their public report of the attack did not keep other people from calling newspapers and law enforcement authorities to report their own giant bird sightings over the days and weeks that followed. The giant birds seemed to be on the move—and they wreaked havoc across the state as they traveled.

On July 28, three days after the Lawndale attack, Janet Brandt was driving home from Minier to Armington and noticed a bird that was larger than the hood of her car. It was at about 5:30 P.M. and she saw the bird flying from east to west in the late-afternoon light. She only saw it for a few moments, flying about thirty feet off the ground, but she did notice that it seemed to have a ring of white around its neck.

Later that same day, at around 8:00 P.M., a McLean County farmer named Stanley Thompson spotted a bird of the same size and description flying over his farm. He, his wife, and several friends were watching some radio-controlled airplanes when the bird flew close to the models. He claimed the bird had a wingspan of at least ten feet across. It dwarfed the small planes that buzzed close to it. He later told McLean County Sheriff's Sergeant Robert Boyd that the bird had about a six-foot-long body and a wingspan that was easily nine feet. Boyd commented that Thompson was a "credible witness." He had lived in the area for a long time and had no reason to make up stories. Boyd had questioned the original reports that came in but after speaking with Thompson, he decided to investigate.

On July 28, Lisa Montgomery of Tremont was washing her car when she looked up and saw a giant bird crossing the sky overhead, soaring slowly over a nearby cornfield. She estimated that it had a seven-foot wingspan and described it as black with a low tail. She said that it disappeared into the sky towards Pekin.

The next sighting took place on July 29 near Bloomington when a mail truck driver named James Majors spotted the two birds. He was driving from Armington to Delevan at 5:30 A.M. when he saw them alongside the highway. He was just passing by a Hampshire hog farm when he spotted the birds overhead. One of the creatures dropped down into a field and extended its claws more than two feet from its body. Suddenly, it snatched up a small animal that Majors believed was a baby pig, which he guessed weighed between forty and sixty pounds. The bird then flapped its wings and soared back into the sky to rejoin the other creature. Both of them flew away to the north. Majors was unable to identify the birds but he had seen condors in California and stated that these birds were larger.

At 2:00 A.M. on Saturday, July 30, Dennis Turner and several friends from Downs reported a monstrous bird perched on a telephone pole. Turner claimed that the bird dropped something near the base of the pole. When police officers investigated the sighting, they found a huge rat near the spot. Several residents of Waynesville reported seeing a black bird with an eight-foot wingspan later that same day.

Reports of giant birds continued to come in from Bloomington and north-central Illinois, and then finally further south, from Decatur to Macon and Sullivan. On July 30, the same day the birds were reported near Bloomington, a writer and construction worker named "Texas John" (now known as "Chief A. J.") Huffer filmed two large birds while fishing at Lake Shelbyville, about two hours to the south.

Huffer was a resident of Tuscola and was spending the day with his son when they both spotted the birds roosting in a tree. Huffer frightened the birds with his boat horn; when they took flight, he managed to shoot one hundred feet of color film. Huffer had experience as a combat photographer with the Marines and was an avid outdoorsman, and he usually kept his 16mm motion-picture camera with him on outings. As he grabbed the camera, he noted that the bird was black and made a kind of "clacking" sound and described its cry as "primeval." Huffer stated recently that he believed the largest bird had a wingspan of eighteen to twenty feet.

Huffer sold a portion of the footage shot that day to the CBS television affiliate in Champaign and it aired later that night during a newscast. After the footage aired, experts were quick to dismiss Huffer's claims, along with the accounts of everyone else who had been reporting huge birds around this time. Officials from the Department of Conservation insisted the birds were merely turkey vultures and were nothing out of the ordinary. These claims were refuted by wildlife experts, however, who stated that no turkey vultures were of the size reported by witnesses.

Unfortunately, no real proof of anything can be obtained from Huffer's footage. Biologists and several other wildlife experts who have seen the film state that it's impossible to tell the size of the birds from the footage. Because much of the footage shows the birds with only the sky as the background, it's hard to see whether the birds are actually as large as Huffer's recollection of them. Even the footage shot with trees as a backdrop is from too far away to ascertain the birds' size. The footage is unquestionably interesting, but it's hard to say just what kind of birds are captured in it.

The sightings of the birds continued. On July 31, Mrs. Albert Dunham of rural Bloomington was on the second floor of her house when she noticed a large dark shadow passing by her window. She quickly realized that it was a giant bird and got a good look at it. Her description was almost identical to others from around that time, and included a white ring around the bird's neck. Her son chased the bird to a nearby landfill, but it had vanished before a local newspaper photographer could get a photo of it.

On August 11, John and Wanda Chappell saw a giant bird land in a tree near their home in Odin. According to the witnesses, it was gray-black with a roughly twelve-foot wingspan. John Chappell stated that it looked like a "prehistoric bird" and that it was likely big enough to have carried away his small daughter if it had wanted to. The huge bird had circled above the Chappells' pond before coming to rest in the tree. John Chappell said that he thought the bird was "so big it had a hard time finding a limb big enough to land on." The Chappells knew the bird had to be heavy because "when it settled in the tree, the tree settled quite a bit," as Wanda Chappell recalled. She and her husband had been having coffee in the kitchen and saw the bird through a sliding glass door. They opened the door carefully, so as to not scare the creature, and called their son to also observe the bird. It stayed in the tree for about five minutes and then soundlessly flew off toward Raccoon Lake and the town of Centralia. Wanda Chappell said that she and her husband almost didn't report the sighting because they were afraid people would think they were crazy.

It's not surprising that they felt this way. The bird sightings of 1977 vanished from the press after the Odin report from John and Wanda Chappell. As the notion appeared in many people's heads that these massive birds could be turkey vultures, interest in the accounts began to fade and many were hesitant to report further sightings for fear of being laughed at, as the Lowe family in Lawndale had been. The stories of further sightings continued, though, and have not died out to this day.

On August 15, 1977, a witness who lived near Herrick reported seeing two giant birds in a forest outside of town. He estimated the wingspans on the creatures to have been at least ten feet. He followed their fligh path to an abandoned barn at the edge of a field where they landed for about five minutes. After that, they vanished into the sky towards Taylorville.

On August 20, Paul Harrold reported a giant bird in the sky near Fairfield. He told me that the bird landed in a field not far from his car and remained there for a few moments before flying off again. According to his report, the bird's wingspan was at least twelve feet. Harrold also stated that he was sure the bird was not a vulture, which are common in Illinois. Having lived out west for several years, he was familiar with large birds but said that he had never seen anything this size.

Another witness said that she had also seen a huge winged creature in 1977. On November 1, she looked out the window of her home near Chester and saw a huge bird resting in the top of a tall tree in her backyard. The bird seemed massive, much larger than anything else she had seen before, and had huge wings that it folded around itself. A few minutes later, it opened its wings and took off into the sky, gliding towards the Mississippi River. Its wingspan, she guessed, was at least ten or fifteen feet. After that, the 1977 Illinois thunderbird sightings came to an end.

What were these creatures? Some will try to convince you that the giant birds that have been seen, and that on rare occasions have carried away children, are nothing more than turkey vultures or condors. In many cases, though, the birds have been spotted by people who would have recognized these common birds, and even if they did not, only a small percentage of the anomalous reports could be so easily dismissed. Some cryptozoological researchers believe that these thunderbirds may be "teratorns," a supposedly extinct bird that once roamed the Americas. If these prehistoric survivors are still around today, they could certainly account for the reports of the giant birds.

But what if some of these winged creatures were something else altogether? In Texas in 1976, witnesses who spotted giant birds were able to use a guide to prehistoric animals to identify the birds they saw as pterodactyls. Another Illinois sighting occurred in late 2003, near Alton and along the Mississippi River. In this case, a hunter stated that he had seen a "big bird" that drifted overhead with "hardly any wing movement" and landed in some trees. He added that it was of huge size and that "I doubted my sanity when I saw it because it looked just like a prehistoric pterodactyl."

We have to be puzzled when we read such tales and wonder about the validity of the strange sightings. Are these mysterious flying creatures actually real? Do they fill the skies of anything other than our imaginations? If they aren't real, then what have so many people seen over the years? Obviously, Illinois' giant birds remain a mystery, but one thing is sure: the sightings have continued over the years and an unusual report occasionally still trickles in from somewhere in the state.

Keep that in mind the next time that you are standing in an open field and a large, dark shadow suddenly fills the sky overhead. Was that just a cloud passing in front of the sun—or something else?

Phantom Attackers

There is no greater phantom attacker in the history of the unexplained in America than the legendary "Mad Gasser of Mattoon," a bizarre figure who wreaked havoc in the small central Illinois town in 1944. This creature turned out to be so elusive that law-enforcement officials eventually declared him nonexistent, despite dozens of eyewitness reports and evidence left behind at the scene of some attacks. Making matters even more interesting, a series of nearly identical attacks took place in Botetourt County, Virginia, in 1933 and 1934. Social scientists declared that the attacks in Mattoon had been nothing more than mass hysteria, but how could the Illinois residents have been able to duplicate the barely publicized events in Virginia?

Both series of attacks involved a mysterious figure, dressed in black, who came and went without warning, left little in the way of clues behind, and for some reason, sprayed a paralyzing gas through the windows of unsuspecting residents. The gas was never identified in either case, both of which took place in fairly isolated areas. The homes that were attacked in Virginia were in a rural county; Mattoon, at that time, was a small town with no large cities in the vicinity. Also, police officials were stumped in both cases.

The story of the Mad Gasser has become known as the greatest mystery in Illinois history. Perhaps what makes this case so infamous is the fact that the central figure remains an enigma. Who (or what) attacked the unsuspecting citizens of Illinois? Was it a mad scientist carrying out some secret experiments? A government agent? A visitor from another planet? No one will ever know for sure, but the annals of the unknown are plagued with cases of attackers who appear and vanish without explanation, prey on the unsuspecting without warning, and then vanish, leaving no trace behind. Could such attackers come from another time and place? Another dimension?

Readers will have to decide such things for themselves, but remember, if the attacks described in the pages that follow happened before in Illinois, they can happen again—perhaps even where you live!

The Mysterious Blue Phantom

The most iconic highway in American and Illinois history is Route 66—the "Mother Road"—which started in Chicago and traveled west to California. Though it no longer officially exists, Route 66 represents a treasure trove of memories and a link to the days of two-lane highways, family vacations, lunches at roadside tables, and little diners that ceased to exist decades ago. It conjures up images of souvenir shops, tourist traps, cozy motor courts, and cheesy roadside attractions that have since crumbled into oblivion. Route 66 makes us think of rusty steel bridges, flickering neon signs, drive-in theaters and more.

Although long stretches of Route 66 still remain today, most of it is a hard-to-define mix of original roadbed, access roads, abandoned fragments, and lost highways. It has been reconfigured in so many ways that even diehard travelers can sometimes become lost and turned around as they try to follow the road's often lonely miles. If you motor along today and begin to wonder if you are still on the old road, watch for abandoned stores, broken and dead neon signs for businesses that have long since vanished, and even creaky motor courts that sometimes still eke out a living from travelers that are now few and far between. It's a place with a lot of lost memories and, for enthusiasts of the strange, a place of some pretty odd tales— including one that has become known as one of the more frightening in highway history.

In the early 1950s, Route 66 in Illinois became a "highway of terror" for many travelers. Someone driving a blue automobile was attacking other automobiles along this road and then, strangest of all, was eluding capture and somehow vanishing without a trace. The identity of the person behind the wheel of what became known as the "Blue Phantom" remains unknown to this day.

The Blue Phantom, as the mysterious driver's automobile was dubbed, first appeared on Route 66 near Joliet in May 1952. Two different drivers independently reported that someone had fired a shot at them from a moving blue automobile. Neither of the drivers was able to get a close look at the car, because it flashed by so quickly, but each of the drivers agreed that a lone man had been behind the wheel. Whoever this man had been, he had fired shots at the cars and one of the drivers had been wounded, although not seriously. The police investigated and could find no connection between the two drivers, nor any enemies who would have wanted to kill the drivers.

Later on the same day of the initial attacks, another driver reported an identical incident—and an identical blue car. This attack took place three miles south of Lincoln, also on Route 66, and state police officers realized that they had a random shooter on their hands, prowling up and down the state's busiest highway.

On June 2, the Blue Phantom's driver changed tactics and ambushed a passing car from outside the infamous vehicle. Edward Smith of St. Louis was driving south on Route 66, just past the Sangamon River, when something struck his car with a loud bang. After slowing down, he looked into his rearview mirror and saw a man run out from some bushes next to the road. He appeared to be carrying a rifle in his hand. The man quickly climbed into a large blue car, which had been hidden out of sight, and roared back north on the highway. Smith guessed that was the vehicle was either a Ford or Buick sedan. He reported the incident to the police, who believed that a .38-caliber bullet had struck Smith's rear window.

On the day of June 8, ten shootings were reported on central Illinois highways. One of the bullets shattered the windshield of a car and all of them were linked to blue automobiles that disappeared without a trace. Miraculously, none of the drivers in the damaged cars were injured. The state police, along with local officers, set up roadblocks along a seventy-five-mile stretch of Route 66. They also hired a small airplane to follow the course of the highway and search for a blue sedan. Owners of ordinary blue automobiles were stopped and often harassed, but no suspects turned up in the search.

On June 9, another Blue Phantom attack occurred near Clinton on Highway 54, which connected to the original highway where attacks had taken place. The driver of the truck that was damaged could not determine the make or model of the car, only that it was blue. He did, however, have two bullet holes in his windshield.

On June 10, the Blue Phantom's driver chose his fifteenth target, still defying all of the police efforts to stop him. This time, he attacked just before dawn, and then led a police officer on a wild chase that exceeded ninety miles per hour. The officer eventually lost the elusive vehicle and stated that he was simply unable to overtake the other car at the speed it was traveling.

A week later, on June 17, the Blue Phantom was off Route 66 again and back on Highway 54. A witness named D. L. Weatherford observed a man standing on a bridge near Mount Pulaski. The man wore a khaki shirt and trousers and was holding a revolver. He was standing next to a blue Chrysler sedan and quickly turned away when Weatherford drove past. Weatherford wisely did not stop to ask questions, but he did report the sighting of the armed man and the blue car to the police. They searched the area but found nothing. Two nights later along the same stretch of road, a blue automobile reportedly opened fire on a Decatur couple and then pursued them south from Mount Pulaski toward Route 66.

On June 24, the Blue Phantom, or at least a vanishing gunman in a blue car, made a last appearance near Champaign, about an hour to the east and some distance from Route 66. On this day, a blue sedan pulled up alongside another car and four shots were fired from the sedan. One of the bullets crashed into the passenger-side window of the other car. The blue sedan quickly sped away and vanished.

After that, the Blue Phantom was lost to history. The incident in Champaign was apparently the last time the driver struck and he was never heard from again. Was the curious car seen by so many a product of mass hysteria, or was some lone nutcase looking for kicks by shooting out people's windows? Either of those options is surely possible—or perhaps the Blue Phantom was something far stranger, something that exists just on the other side of the unknown.

Illinois Vampires

Traditional vampire stories are not common in American history. European vampires, the blood-sucking monsters of nightmare tales, do not often appear in the stories that were told in the American colonies. Most American "vampire" outbreaks could be traced to epidemics of tuberculosis or the "white death," as it was called. The symptoms of tuberculosis, which often wiped out entire families in the 1800s, mirrored the wasting away, paleness, and death of vampire legends. A vampire, which seemed quite real to the early settlers, was a death-bringer and a monster to be feared.

Tales of such vampires often brought terror to unsuspecting communities, especially in New England and along the Atlantic Seaboard, but few traveled as far west as Illinois. In the Midwest, residents told tales of different kinds of night creatures that were perhaps even stranger than their eastern counterparts.

A short distance over the Illinois border is the quiet Wisconsin town of Mineral Point, which in 1981 had vampire problems. Residents were constantly calling the police to report a man, described as being six feet tall and having a white face, who jumped out at people from dark and shadowy places, clad in a black cape. Skeptical at first, officers were soon convinced by the sheer number of calls they received that something weird was going on.

On March 30, Officer Jon Pepper was on duty when he saw a man "dressed like Dracula" lurking behind some tombstones in the city cemetery. Pepper approached the man and asked him what he was doing. The figure immediately stood up and Pepper guessed him to be at least six feet, five inches tall. Whoever the strange man was, he said nothing, but immediately turned and began to run. He quickly outdistanced the officer and when the figure jumped over a four-foot barbed-wire fence, Pepper called off the chase. The "vampire" vanished into the darkness. Soon after, the department stationed extra officers at the cemetery; several more sightings took place, but they were unable to capture the mysterious man. Eventually, the sightings came to an end and the story of the "Mineral Point Vampire" has largely been forgotten.

But Illinois has its own vampire tales. In the middle and late 1970s, a mysterious figure was reported in the area of St. Casimir's Cemetery on the South Side of Chicago. The first sighting occurred in 1978 when a man was driving past the cemetery on Pulaski Road and spotted a figure standing just inside the cemetery fence, draped in a long, black cape. The figure had its back to the road, but the driver slowed his car to get a better look. As he did, the man behind the gate turned around to face him, revealing a ghastly white face above the neck of the cloak. The sinister-looking man bared his teeth at the driver and the fellow in the car sped off.

On June 14 and 15, the figure was seen again, this time by neighborhood teenagers, who added that he was not only wearing the long cape, but also had a top hat on his head. He seemingly vanished without explanation whenever he was approached. The local police believed that the macabre antics of the man were nothing more than a prank meant to frighten the local children, but they became concerned after reports stated that the man had approached, chased, and threatened youths on two separate occasions. According to the accounts, the man was "six feet tall, extremely thin with broken teeth and wearing dirty, muddy clothing." Both reports also said that he had a "disgusting odor" about him, to go along with the hat, cape, and makeup—if it was actually makeup, that is.

Stories about the sightings began to make the rounds. Motorists traveling southbound on Kostner Avenue near the cemetery arrived at the stoplight at 111th Street with their headlights illuminating the front gates of the cemetery. Many of them claimed to see a thin man with a pale face, dressed in black and wearing a cape, peering out at them from the graveyard. The man apparently disappeared before the traffic light changed. Others who were walking or riding a bicycle past the gates stated that they saw the same figure. Some even added that they heard a menacing hiss or a growl before the "vampire" disappeared. A few noted that he would reach out at them through the gate, his fingers curling into claws.

One of the most frightening encounters with the St. Casimir's Vampire took place in 1979. A woman was driving south on 115th Street, approaching the railroad tracks on the western edge of Restvale Cemetery. She stated later that a man who matched the earlier, vampire-like descriptions suddenly appeared on the street in front of her car. To avoid hitting the man, she swerved into oncoming traffic and then veered back into her own lane. She immediately stopped and looked in the rearview mirror but the man was gone. There was no place where he could have hidden, she insisted—he simply vanished.

Another encounter took place in the backyard of the home of an elderly woman who lived near the cemetery. She opened the sliding patio door to let her dog outside. No sooner had the poodle stepped out than it began to bark loudly. The startled woman switched on the back patio light to see what was bothering the dog and was terrified to see a figure lying in the grass. He immediately turned and she got a long look at his white face and bared teeth. He let out a loud hiss and then got up and began to run. According to her statement, he then jumped over a four-foot fence without even touching it. When he landed on the other side, he vanished into the darkness.

Who was this strange creature and why did he appear near the cemetery gates? No one knew then or has ever offered a credible explanation for his behavior. It's been more than thirty years since the St. Casimir's Vampire prowled the streets of Chicago's South Side, but some older people in the area have never forgotten when it was terrifying to pass by the cemetery at night. Keep a watchful eye when you pass by those cemetery gates, they say: you never know if the vampire may have come back.

Most people will tell you that vampires exist only in the pages of horror novels or on the silver screen, but there are those in Illinois who insist that at least one such creature is very real: the Spring Valley Vampire. This mysterious creature, clad all in black, has been rumored to linger in the Old Lithuanian Cemetery, just outside of Spring Valley, for many years. Stories tell of him hiding among the tombstones, preying on local cats and dogs, and terrifying anyone who dares cross through the cemetery after dark.

Even in the daylight, the graveyard can be a foreboding place, and legend tells of the torn and broken bodies of stray animals that have been found, drained of blood, near the old Massock Mausoleum. This tomb is the final resting place of the Massock brothers, once well-known butchers and businessmen in the Spring Valley area.

According to the stories, the mausoleum is the lair of the vampire and it is there that he hides during the daylight hours, only emerging after the sun goes down. In 1967, two local teenagers broke open the tomb, vandalized it, and stole the skull from one of the bodies inside. They were later caught and punished, but their desecration of the crypt only provided new life for the horrifying stories that had been told about the graveyard for years. The arrests sparked reports of new incidents and vampire sightings at the cemetery.

In the early 1980s, the story of the Spring Valley Vampire got the attention of a man who described himself as a "hardened Vietnam veteran" and he decided to take some friends and go out and see if the stories about the monster were true. They drove to the cemetery and then started through the darkness toward the Massock tomb. As they approached it, they were startled to see someone moving in the shadows. A tall, thin figure, draped all in black and "radiating evil," as they described it, shambled toward them. The veteran, who had brought a handgun along on the outing, pulled out the gun and reportedly shot the creature five times at point-blank range. He later stated that the bullets had absolutely no effect on it. The figure hissed and growled and lurched towards them, sending the man and his friends fleeing from the graveyard in panic.

Word spread about the incident and eventually, some researchers in Chicago heard the story and decided to come to Spring Valley and check out the cemetery. The group arrived one afternoon about a month after the incident. Walking through the cemetery grounds in the daylight, they studied the Massock mausoleum, searching for a way to gain easy access. The door was securely locked and sealed, but one member of the group poked a stick into a small vent on the side of the crypt. He was startled when something "black and wormy" shot out from the hole and twisted onto the ground. Unnerved, the investigators took off running.

They eventually gathered their courage and returned to the cemetery at dusk. They brought a bottle of holy water with them and emptied it into the vent. They were startled to hear what they described as a "painful groaning" coming from inside and the group once again fled the cemetery. This time they did not return, and they decided to leave the Spring Valley Vampire to someone else.

Since that time, there have been other reports of the cemetery's vampire. In spite of this, many in the area don't take the story seriously and believe it's nothing more than the product of tall tales and overactive imaginations—but not everyone feels that way.

According to "Joan," who did not want her last name used for reasons that will soon become obvious, the Spring Valley Vampire is very real. She knows this because she encountered the creature face-to-face one night back in 1960.

Joan was only twelve years old at the time and was over at a friend's house one summer night. She lived close to the cemetery and her friend's house was several blocks away. Joan often took a shortcut through the graveyard when she was walking home. This is exactly what she did on this particular night, but this time, she was coming home much later than usual. Darkness had already fallen and she knew that she was likely going to get in trouble with her mother for getting home so late. She later recalled that this was the only thing on her mind that night as she hurried through the cemetery.

Joan walked quickly among the tombstones, pondering what excuse she was going to give her mother when she arrived at home, when suddenly she was knocked to the ground! In an interview that she granted more than forty-five years after the incident, she told of how she was hit very hard in the back and shoved down onto the ground. She had not heard anyone approaching her and had seen no one else in the cemetery. When her eyes focused, though, she saw a figure standing over her that was exceedingly tall and gaunt. The figure bent down towards her from the waist and she saw that it was man with a set of very long, yellow, sharp teeth. The experience, she said, was so "surreal and unsettling" that she is unable to remember what happened next. All she knows is that the figure was there one moment and then gone the next. She couldn't even remember how she got home that night, what her mother said to her, or going to bed.

However, she does recall waking up the next morning, getting dressed, and going back to the cemetery to look for some evidence that the strange, foggy incident actually took place. It had rained the day before and the ground had been soft, so it was easy for her to find her own footprints in the wet soil. She could see where she entered the graveyard and where the ground was disturbed when she had been pushed down, but nothing else. The other person, whoever he had been, had left no footprints behind.

What, or who, did Joan encounter that night in 1960? Was it a vampire, or at least a mysterious figure of some sort, that lurked in the Spring Valley cemetery? No one can definitively say, but even after all of these years, Joan maintains that the incident really occurred.

"What I can tell you are the things that happened to me," she said. "I know they are true."

The Mad Gasser of Mattoon

Illinois is a place of weird stories and strange tales, including bizarre histories of phantom attackers and inexplicable events. But there is no story stranger than that of the "Mad Gasser," a phantom who wreaked havoc for a time and then seemingly vanished, leaving behind no clue as to the purpose or motives behind the strange acts he committed.

Was the enigmatic Mad Gasser truly, as some have suggested, a presence that had the ability to step from one dimension to another, only to disappear again to another place and time? Or were his actions easier to explain? Was he merely some odd loner with a penchant for science who somehow managed to avoid capture while he carried out his strange experiment? That, unfortunately, is a question that has never been, and probably never will be, adequately answered.

The Mad Gasser arrived in Mattoon in 1944, but it's unlikely that this was the first time that he wreaked havoc on an unsuspecting community. To truly understand what happened in Illinois, we have to travel hundreds of miles to Virginia and revisit a series of attacks that occurred eleven years before the events in Mattoon. As the reader will soon see, the similarity between the events is almost undoubtedly not a coincidence.

In 1933, Virginia's Botetourt County was a quiet area that had never really experienced much out of the ordinary. That all began to change on December 22, when the home of Mrs. and Mrs. Cal Huffman, near Haymakertown, was attacked by a mysterious figure that was unlike anything previously seen, or even heard of, in the region.

At around 10 o'clock that evening, Mrs. Huffman stated that she grew nauseated after smelling a strange gas that had apparently been sprayed into her house. She decided to go on to bed, but her husband remained awake and alert to see if the lurker who had sprayed the gas might return. A half hour later, another wave of gas filled the room and Huffman immediately went to the home of his landlord, K. W. Henderson. The Huffman home was located on the Henderson property and was only a short distance away from the main house. Huffman telephoned the police from the landlord's house. An Officer Lemon was dispatched to the scene and he stayed until around midnight. Immediately after he left, another gas attack was launched on the property, filling both floors of the Huffman house. All eight members of the Huffman family, along with Ashby Henderson, were affected by the gas. Ashby and Cal Huffman had been keeping watch for the return of the prowler and thought that they saw a man running away after the attack.

According to reports, the gas caused the victims to become very nauseated, gave them a headache, and caused mouth and throat muscles to restrict. Alice, the Huffmans' nineteen-year-old daughter, was most affected by the gas and she had to be given artificial respiration in order to revive her. She experienced convulsions for some time afterward. Her doctor, S. F. Driver, later reported that while part of her condition was caused by extreme nervousness over the attack, he had no doubt that the gas attack was responsible for the fact that her condition continued.

However, no one could determine what kind of gas was used; Dr. W. N. Breckinridge, who assisted with the police investigation, ruled out ether, chloroform, and tear gas. Nor could they determine who had sprayed it into the house. The only clue that Officer Lemon found at the scene was the print of a woman's shoe beneath the window through which the attacker was thought to have sprayed the gas.

The next attack took place in the Botetourt County town of Cloverdale. Clarence Hall, his wife, and their two children came home from a church service at around 9:00 P.M. on Christmas Eve. Five minutes after they entered the house, they smelled a strange odor. Hall went into one of the back rooms to investigate and came back moments later, staggering and swaying. His wife, who also felt nauseated and weak, had to drag him outside. The effects of the gas did not linger with Mr. Hall, but Mrs. Hall experienced eye irritation for the next two days. Dr. Breckinridge again helped the police and he noted that the gas "tasted sweet" and that he detected a trace of formaldehyde in it. He still had no idea what type of gas it actually was, though, and investigators again found only one clue at the scene. Apparently, a nail had been pulled from one of the windows. Police officers surmised that perhaps the attacker had sprayed the gas through the hole that had been opened up.

Another attack occurred on December 27 when Troutville welder A. L. Kelly and his mother were sprayed in their home. Oddly, the police learned that a man and a woman in a 1933 Chevrolet had been seen driving back and forth in front of Kellys' house around the time of the attack. A neighbor managed to get a partial plate number on the car but the police were unable to locate it.

No attacks took place over the next two weeks but on January 10, the gasser struck again at the home of Homer Hylton, near Haymakertown. Hylton and his wife were upstairs asleep and their daughter, a Mrs. Moore, was sleeping downstairs while her husband was out of town on business. Around 10:00 P.M., she got up to attend to her baby and later recalled that she heard mumbling voices outside and someone fiddling with the window. She claimed that moments later, the room filled with gas. As she grabbed her child, she experienced a "marked feeling of numbness." The window where the noises came from had been slightly broken for some time and this may have allowed the Gasser access to the house. It was later suggested that Mrs. Moore was not a gas attack victim at all, but that her "symptoms" were merely nervousness and fear caused by what she thought were voices, but was actually wind that was blowing through a crack in the window glass. Unfortunately, this theory does not hold up when considering the fact that a neighbor, G. E. Poage, also heard voices around the same time.

Also on January 10, Troutville resident G. D. Kinzie was attacked. This case was not reported until later and was different from the others. Dr. Driver's investigation concluded that chlorine was the gas used in the attack. Chlorine was then mentioned in several subsequent accounts until a Roanoke chemistry professor later ruled it out as a possible cause.

After a few quiet nights, the Gasser returned on January 16, this time attacking the home of F. B. Duval near Bonsack. Duval left the house to summon the police and as he reached a nearby intersection, saw a man run up to a parked car, get in, and speed away. He and Officer Lemon spent several hours driving around searching for the car, but they found nothing. The next day, Lemon again found the prints of a woman's shoes, this time where the car had been parked.

On January 19, the Gasser struck again. This time, gas was sprayed through the window of a Mrs. Campbell, a former judge's wife, who lived near Cloverdale. She was sitting near the window in question; moments after seeing the shade move, she became sick.

A few nights later, the gas attacks reached their peak, with five attacks taking place over a period of three nights. The first attack took place on January 21 when Howard Crawford and his wife returned to their home between Cloverdale and Troutville. Mr. Crawford went into the house first to light a lamp but quickly came stumbling back out. He was overwhelmed by the gas, which Dr. Driver again said was chlorine. Police officers were again able to find only a single clue at the house, this time the crank of an old automobile. The metal crank seemed to have absolutely nothing to do with the attack, but it was simply too strange an item to be left behind. On the other hand, it was also too common of an item in those days to be traced.

On January 22, three separate attacks occurred in Carvin's Cove. In just one hour's time, the Gasser covered a distance of about two miles, attacking the homes of Ed Reedy, George C. Riley, and Raymond Etter. The victims in each house claimed to have numbness and nausea. Riley called his brother, a Roanoke police officer, and a blockade of the nearby roads was quickly put into place. Although the Gasser managed to elude the authorities, one of Mr. Etter's sons claimed to have seen a figure disappearing from the direction of the house. He gave chase and even fired a few shots at the man from a distance of thirty yards, but he got away.

On January 23, Mrs. R. H. Hartsell and her family spent the night with some neighbors. When they returned to their Pleasantdale Church home at 4:30 A.M., they discovered that the house had been filled with gas. For some bizarre reason, someone had also piled wood and brush up against their front door during the night. The only possible motive for this would have been to keep the family from easily escaping once the house was filled with gas. This means that the elusive Gasser likely believed the family was home at the time of the attack.

This new series of gassings had the entire community in an uproar. Families who lived in more isolated areas began spending the night with friends and neighbors, hoping to find security in numbers. Men armed with shotguns and rifles began patrolling the roadways at night. The local newspaper, the *Roanoke Times*, stated that it was sure the gassers would be caught and it pleaded with the farmers not to shoot anyone.

The authorities were growing more concerned. They had previously believed the gassings had been nothing more than pranks played by some mischievous boys. Now the county sheriff's office was forced to admit that if this had been the case, the boys would have been caught long before. They had begun to investigate the idea that a mentally deranged person might be the culprit, perhaps even an unhinged victim of the World War I gas attacks.

On January 25, the Gasser may have attempted to strike again, but this time was foiled. Around 9:00 P.M., a dog at the home of Chester Snyder began barking. Alerted, Snyder jumped out of bed and grabbed his shotgun. Darting outside, he ran across the yard and fired a shot at a man that he saw creeping along a ditch about twenty feet from the house. The shot apparently missed and Snyder only had one shell in his gun. He ran back inside for more ammunition but by the time he returned, the man was gone.

Snyder called the police and a deputy sheriff named Zimmerman investigated the scene. He managed to find footprints that led from the road to the ditch and signs that the prowler had hidden behind a tree on the property for some time before the dog sounded the alarm. More tracks led from the tree to the house and then stopped, marking the point where the man had retreated. Visitors who had left the Snyder home a short time earlier recalled seeing a man about a half mile away on the road. There was, of course, no real evidence to say that the prowler was actually the Gasser, but based on the events that had been occurring, any sort of incident like this was immediately suspicious.

On January 28, the Gasser managed to pull off another attack, this time at the Cloverdale home of Ed Stanley. Stanley, his wife, and three other adults were all affected by the still mysterious gas. Frank Guy, a hired hand on the farm, ran outside immediately after the gas filled the house and later stated that he saw four men running away in the direction of the Blue Ridge Mountains. He ran back inside to get his gun and when he returned to the yard, he couldn't see the fleeing figures, but he could hear them in the woods. He fired several shots in the direction of the voices but felt that it was unlikely that he hit anything.

The Gasser returned two nights later and attacked the Stanley house again. This time, however, Stanley heard a sound outside the window before the attack took place. What happened after that remains a mystery, as no further details were reported in the contemporary accounts.

The last of what were likely authentic gas attacks took place at the home of A. P. Skaggs in Nace, two miles from Troutville, on February 3. Skaggs and his wife, along with five other adults, were all affected by the gas. The group was so badly hurt by the gas that Sheriff Williamson would tell the skeptics who later scoffed at the gassing cases, "No amount of imagination in the world would make people as ill as the Skaggses are."

The final attack on the Skaggs family was as dramatic as the first attack on the Huffman family. It's thought that perhaps the Gasser wanted to mark his entrance and exit with large attacks. In both instances, it seemed as though the gas was sprayed into the houses two times on the night of the attacks, although investigator Lemon stated that he believed lingering gas near the ceiling could have been responsible for what seemed to be a separate attack. The gas had some pretty strange effects on the people in the house and on the family dog as well. One of the Skaggses' nephews began screaming and flailing about, crying that he was "trapped in the house." The following day, Officer Lemon was at the scene and one of the children came in weeping that the dog was dying. Lemon went out and saw that the animal was rolling over and over in the snow, just as dogs do when they are sprayed by a skunk. As no skunk odor was present, this certainly seemed odd. It was later reported that the dog was sick for some time after and the formerly well-trained animal refused to pay attention to commands for some time after the incident.

There were no more credible accounts of gas attacks in the county after this, but there was plenty of hysteria. During the following week, there were twenty attacks reported in nearby Roanoke County and a number of other reports in Lexington, about thirty miles away. And while a few of the later "attacks" may have been genuine, they lacked the detail of the original incidents and most were likely hysterical reactions to ordinary odors or the result of hoaxes perpetrated by pranksters. In one of these hoaxes, a teenager threw a bottle of insecticide into a woman's window; a similar incident on February 9 gave the police and the newspapers the opportunity to declare that the Gasser mystery was over.

The last "insecticide" case did have some interesting aspects to it, however. At the time when J. G. Shafer of Lithia believed his house was gassed on February 9, he went outside and scooped up some snow that contained a sweet-smelling substance. It was analyzed and was determined to contain sulfur, arsenic, and mineral oil, all of which were commonly used in insecticide sprays. This caused the police to dismiss the attack as a hoax, but some investigators weren't so sure. Strangely, police officers found footprints leading from the front porch of the house to the barn, but no trail that led away from that building. It was as if whoever had been on the porch had then walked into the barn and simply vanished. Also, as with some of the other earlier cases, a "woman's tracks" led from the yard to the road.

The later cases led the general public to swallow the unconvincing theory that faulty chimney flues and wild imaginations had caused the entire affair. That explanation was never accepted by those who were attacked and certain police officers involved, such as investigator Lemon. In hindsight, the later cases helped to show that the original attacks were not merely hysteria. The later incidents did not follow the pattern of the original attacks; they occurred outside of the already established area, took place at no particular times, and did not cause any lasting physical effects. It should also be noted that the original attacks, while taking place in Botetourt County, were spread out enough throughout the area that neighbors could not infect one another with hysteria.

So if mass hysteria was not the answer in the Mad Gasser of Botetourt County case, then could a natural explanation have been to blame? This also seems unlikely. Explanations like pollution and faulty chimney flues don't hold up when looking at all of the factors in the case, including the selection of victims, times of the attacks, thorough police investigations, and of course, the fleeing figure or figures that were seen running away from the residences in question. The hoaxer, or even the lone lunatic, theories are not much better either. Even though a mysterious figure was often seen, there were never any useful clues left behind and the identity of the Gasser was never discovered.

It was almost as if the strange figure left Virginia and vanished without a trace, never to return again. And while perhaps the Gasser did not return to Botetourt County, could he have possibly surfaced in Illinois eleven years later?

Mattoon, like Botetourt County had been, was a pretty uneventful place in 1944. Located in the southeastern section of central Illinois, it was a quiet, typical Midwestern town of the era. But what happened there in 1944 was anything but typical. The events that occurred placed the small farming community under the scrutiny of the entire country and would one day be called a textbook case of mass hysteria. But was it really? To dismiss the entire case as nothing more than wild imaginations run amok, the authorities and psychologists had to ignore not only credible witness statements, but actual physical evidence as well. The case of the "Mad Gasser of Mattoon" simply cannot be so easily ignored.

The weird events in the case began during the early-morning hours of August 31, 1944. A local man was startled out of a deep sleep, sitting up in his bed and loudly crying out. His wife was awakened and questioned him about what was wrong. He told her that he felt very sick and asked her if she was sure that she had turned off the gas in the kitchen. The lightheadedness that he was feeling, along with extreme nausea, were very similar to what he might have felt if exposed to household gas. His wife quickly agreed to get up and check the pilot light on the stove, but to her surprise, found that she was unable to move. Her entire body was paralyzed from the chest down. Around the same time, according to accounts collected later, a woman in a neighboring home also tried to get out of bed and discovered that she too was paralyzed.

The following evening, September 1, Mrs. Bert Kearney was awakened by a peculiar, stifling odor in her bedroom. It was sweet and overpowering and as it grew stronger, she began to feel a tingling feeling of numbness in her legs and lower body. Frightened, she tried to get out of bed, only to discover that she was unable to move. She screamed and her cries alerted her neighbors, who called the police. The following day, Mrs.

Kearney was still feeling the effects of the gas. She complained of burned lips, a parched mouth and throat, and a terrible thirst that she couldn't quench. The police, along with some concerned neighbors, searched the Kearney yard, but found nothing out of the ordinary.

But this was not the last strange incident at this home.

Later on that same evening, near midnight, Bert Kearney returned home from work, completely unaware of what had happened in his home that night. As he turned his car into the driveway, he spotted a man lurking near the house. Kearney's description of the Mad Gasser would fit those given by later eyewitnesses. The man was tall and wearing dark or black clothing and a tight-fitting cloth cap. Kearney spotted him standing near a window at the side of the house. When the headlights from the approaching car illuminated him, the man ran away. Kearney, shocked and angry, jumped out of the car and pursued him, but the prowler got away. Returning to the house, Kearney called the police and finally learned of the strange incidents that had already taken place that night.

The incidents at the Kearney home, as well as the earlier gas attack, soon became public knowledge. Mattoon was not yet panicked, but people were very concerned. The story was badly handled by the authorities, and the local newspaper reported the first attacks, as well as subsequent ones, in a wildly sensational manner. Years later, debunkers of the case would blame the newspaper for manufacturing the hysteria involving the Gasser. Frightened small-town folks, the skeptics said, took leave of their senses after reading the lurid newspaper accounts and imagined that a "mad gasser" was wreaking havoc on the community. In some ways, and for some of the later accounts, this may be a plausible explanation for what happened in 1944—but it certainly does not eliminate all of the evidence that says something truly bizarre took place in Mattoon.

By the morning of September 5, the Mattoon Police Department had received reports of four more gas attacks. The details in each of these attacks were eerily similar, even though none of the witnesses knew that any other incidents had taken place that day. Each attack was described in almost exactly the same way (adding details not included in the newspaper) and each victim complained of a sickeningly sweet odor that caused them to become ill and partially paralyzed for up to thirty minutes.

Later that night, September 5, the first physical evidence of the gasser's existence was discovered at the home of Carl and Beulah Cordes. To this day, no one has any idea what these clues might mean. The Cordeses were returning home that night from dinner with friends when they found a white cloth lying on their porch, directly in front of the door. Mrs. Cordes picked it up and noticed a strange odor coming from it. She held it closer to her nose, hoping to identify the smell, and suddenly felt light-headed and sick to her stomach. Her knees buckled and she almost fainted on the porch. Acting quickly, Carl grabbed her and helped her into the house. Beulah sank down onto the couch, but her symptoms worsened. Her lips and face began to swell, as if from an allergic reaction, and her mouth began to bleed. The symptoms did not subside for more than two hours. Worried, Carl Cordes called the police and officers were dispatched to investigate. Another search of the porch was conducted and officers sound a skeleton key and an empty lipstick tube, neither of which belonged to the Cordeses. Both items were taken into evidence, along with the white cloth.

Police wanted to write off incident as an attempted break-in by a prowler that was frightened off by the Cordeses returning home, but they couldn't ignore the cloth that had caused such peculiar symptoms in Mrs. Cordes. It seemed connected to the other gas attacks, but it should be noted that Mrs. Cordes displayed symptoms that were different from those experienced by the other victims. She did become sick to her stomach but there were no sensations of paralysis. In addition, if this was the gasser's work, why did he try to get into the house rather than just spray gas into a window? The Cordeses, like just about everyone else in Mattoon during the warm end-of-summer nights, had left windows open. Could the gasser's intentions have been different during this attack?

Two hours later, also on September 5, the gasser struck again. This time, he followed the same methods used in the earlier attacks, spraying gas into an open window. He did not try to break into the house and in fact, there would only be one other report that even hinted that the attacker tried to get into a house. In that incident, a woman claimed that a person in dark clothing tried to force open her front door.

The attacks continued over the course of the next five days. Mattoon residents were now reporting glimpses of the gasser. In every report, he was described as being a tall, thin man in dark clothes and a tight black cap. The description never varied, even though the witnesses who provided it came from different parts of town. Up to that point, it had not been mentioned in the newspaper accounts. If the gasser was merely a figment of the townspeople's imaginations, how were they all describing him in the same way?

As more and more attacks were reported, the harried police department did its best to respond to the mysterious crimes. Eventually, the authorities summoned two FBI agents from Springfield to look into the case, but their presence did nothing to discourage the strange reports. Panic was beginning to grip the city and rumors circulated that the gasser was an escapee from an insane asylum or a German spy who was testing out some sort of poisonous gas. Armed citizens took to the streets, organizing watches and patrols in hopes of stopping attacks that continued to happen anyway. In fact, despite the armed patrols, the gas attacks became more frequent and definitely less careful. The gasser was now leaving behind footprints and sliced window screens at the scene. This should have made him easier to catch, but it didn't.

A local citizens' "vigilance group" did manage to arrest one suspect, but he was released after he passed a polygraph test. Local businessmen announced that they would be holding a mass protest rally on Saturday, September 9, to put more pressure on the already pressured Mattoon police force. The Mad Gasser was now becoming more than just a threat to public safety; he was now a political liability and a stain on the public image of the city.

The gasser, undeterred by armed vigilantes and political protests, continued his attacks. Mrs. Violet Driskell and her daughter, Ramona, were awakened on September 9 by the sound of someone removing the storm sash on their bedroom window. They got out of bed and tried to hurry outside for help, but the fumes overcame Ramona and she fell to the floor. With her eyes streaming tears from the sickly gas odor, she began throwing up. Mrs. Driskell stated that she saw a man running away from the house.

A short time later that night, the Gasser sprayed fumes into the partially opened window of a room where Mrs. Russell Bailey, Katherine Tuzzo, and Mrs. Genevieve Haskell and her young son were sleeping. At another home, Miss Frances Smith, the principal of the Columbian Grade School, and her sister, Maxine, were also overwhelmed with gas and fell ill. They both reported partial paralysis in their legs and arms and experienced choking and nausea. They also added something new to the case: They claimed that as the sweet odor began to fill the room, they heard a buzzing noise from outside, which they believed was the gasser's "spraying apparatus" in operation.

By Sunday, September 10, Mad Gasser panic had peaked. FBI agents were trying to determine the type of gas being used in the attacks and the police department was trying not only to find the gasser, but also to keep the armed citizens off the streets. Neither law-enforcement agency was having much luck with any of these tasks. By the following Saturday night, several dozen well-armed farmers from the surrounding area had joined the patrols in Mattoon. In spite of this, six attacks still took place, including the three just mentioned. Another couple, Mr. and Mrs. Stewart B. Scott, returned to their farm on the edge of Mattoon late in the evening to find the house filled with sweet-smelling gas.

The following Monday morning, September 11, seemed to mark a turning point in the case. It was almost as if the idea of the gas attacks moving from the city of Mattoon to the rural area outside of town had become something too hard to believe. Official acceptance of the attacks was now over. In the words of Thomas V. Wright, the City Commissioner of Public Health: "There is no doubt that a gas maniac exists and has made a number of attacks. But many of the reported attacks are nothing more than hysteria. Fear of the gas man is entirely out of proportion to the menace of the relatively harmless gas he is spraying. The whole town is sick with hysteria and last night it spread out into the country."

When city officials started doubting the validity of the "Mad Gasser," so did the newspaper. Subsequent news accounts began to take on a more skeptical tone. Despite believable claims by new victims and physical evidence left behind, the police began dismissing reports of attacks and started suggesting to complainants that they were imagining things. At this point, there was little else that the authorities could do. The Mad Gasser, if he existed at all, could not be caught, identified, or tracked down. Officials started to believe that if they ignored the problem, it would just go away. After all, if the man were real, how could he have possibly escaped detection for so long?

Psychologists theorized that the women of Mattoon had simply dreamed up the gasser as a desperate cry for attention, as many of their husbands were overseas fighting in the war. Women did, they stated, easily become hysterical, especially when their men were not around to protect them. Of course, this so-called theory ignored the fact that many of the victims and witnesses were men and that the "imaginary" gasser was leaving behind evidence of his existence.

Unfortunately for the police, the gasser was not interested in the fact that he had been dismissed as imaginary. He continued with his attacks. On the night of Monday, September 11, the police received a number of reports of new attacks; after half-hearted attempts to investigate, they dismissed all of them as false alarms. Just days before, a crime specialist with the State Department of Public Safety named Richard T. Piper had told reporters, "This is one of the strangest cases I have ever encountered in my years of police work," but now new calls were only worthy of perfunctory examination. This was in spite of the fact that a doctor who appeared on the scene shortly after one of the evening's attacks stated that there had been a "peculiar odor" in the room. Officials were just no longer interested.

Mattoon Police Chief C. E. Cole issued what he felt was the final statement on the gas attacks on September 12. He stated that large quantities of carbon tetrachloride gas were used at the local Atlas Diesel Engine Company and that this gas must be causing the reported cases of illness and paralysis. It could be carried throughout the town on the wind and could have left the stains that were found on the rag at one of the homes. As for the Mad Gasser himself, well, he was simply a figment of the victims' imaginations. The whole case, Cole said, "was a mistake from beginning to end."

Not surprisingly, a spokesman for the Atlas Diesel Engine plant was quick to deny the allegations that his company had caused the incidents in town, maintaining that the only use for that gas in the plant was in their fire extinguishers. Any similar gases used at the plant weren't capable of being carried on the wind in the manner suggested by Chief Cole. It should be noted that no gases from the plant had ever been blamed for anything out of the ordinary in Mattoon. In addition, how was poison gas wafting through the air supposed to cut window screens and leave footprints behind at homes where people were experiencing nausea and paralysis?

The official explanation also failed to address the identical descriptions of the gasser that had been given to the police by multiple witnesses. It also neglected to explain how different witnesses managed to report seeing a man of the gasser's description fleeing the scene of an attack, even when the witness had no idea that an attack had taken place.

Mattoon's final Mad Gasser attack took place on Wednesday, September 13, at the home of Mrs. Bertha Bench and her son, Orville. They described the attacker as a woman who was dressed in man's clothing and who sprayed gas into a bedroom window. The next morning, footprints that appeared to have been made by a woman's shoes were found in the dirt below the window. And while this report does not match any of the earlier attacks in Mattoon (except for perhaps the empty tube of lipstick that was found on the Cordes's porch), readers will recognize the claims of a woman's shoe prints from several attacks in Botetourt County in 1933.

After September 13, 1944, the Mad Gasser of Mattoon was never seen or heard from again.

The real story behind what happened in Mattoon and Botetourt County is still unknown and it's unlikely that we will ever know what was behind these weird events. The two cases cannot be dismissed as imaginary, for it seems certain that something did take place in both locations, however strange it might have been. Was the Mad Gasser real? And if he was, who was he? And if he was real, could he have been the same figure in both cases? It's hard to ignore the similarities between the two cases, from his method of operation to the unusual style of the attacks. In Virginia, the gasser was not always reported as being alone, as he was in Mattoon; but then again, what about the identical reports of prints left by a woman's shoe?

Many believe that the Mattoon attacks may have been "copycat" attacks based on the earlier Virginia attacks. While this seems unlikely, based on the fact that the Botetourt stories were not widely reported outside of the area, it could be possible. It's also possible that the Mattoon and Virginia attacks have no connection at all and their similarities are only a bizarre coincidence.

In 1944, it was suggested that the Mattoon gasser was anything from a mad scientist to an "ape-man," and researchers today have their own theories, some valid and some just as wild.

Could the Mad Gasser have been an agent of our own government, who came to an obscure Midwestern town to test some military gas that could be used in the war effort? It might be telling that once national attention came to Mattoon, the authorities began a policy of complete denial and the attacks suddenly ceased.

Could he have been some sort of extraterrestrial visitor using some sort of paralyzing agent to further a hidden agenda? Or could he have been, as some have suggested, a visitor from a dimension outside of our own, thus explaining his ability to appear and disappear at will? Was he a creature so outside the realm of our imaginations that we will never be able to comprehend his motives or the reason that he came to Mattoon?

Or perhaps he was a simply an odd inventor who was testing a new apparatus. Interestingly, I received a letter in 2002 from a woman who explained to me that her father grew up in Mattoon during the time when the gas attacks were taking place. He told her that there had been two sisters living in town at the time who had a brother that was an accomplished chemistry student and who was also allegedly insane. Apparently, a number of people in town believed that he was the gasser because many of the attacks were clustered around his home. Rumor had it that his sisters, fearing reprisal from some of the locals if word got out that he was carrying out the gas attacks, locked him in the basement of their home until they could find a mental institution to put him in. After the young man was sent away, the rumors claimed, the sisters actually carried out several more gas attacks to throw suspicion off their brother. This would explain why heel prints from women's shoes were found and why Bertha and Orville Bench described the gasser as "a woman dressed as a man." Soon after the incident at the Bench house, the attacks stopped.

Whoever, or whatever, he was, the Mad Gasser has vanished into time and is only a memory in the world of the unknown. And perhaps the debunkers were right; perhaps he was never in Mattoon at all. Or perhaps he was simply, as Donald M. Johnson wrote in the 1954 issue of the *Journal of Abnormal and Social Psychology*, a "shadowy manifestation of some unimaginable unknown."

Then again, perhaps he wasn't. Perhaps the Mad Gasser was exactly what we most fear that he was—a mysterious, unimaginable monster that brought our fears of helplessness and the unknown to life.

BIBLIOGRAPHY

Bartholomew, Robert. "Phantom Menace." *Fortean Times* 131 (March 2000).

Blackman, W. Haden. *Field Guide to North American Monsters*. New York: Three Rivers Press, 1998.

Bord, Janet, and Colin Bord. *Alien Animals*. Mechanicsburg, PA: Stackpole Books, 1981.

Clark, Jerome. *Unexplained!* Detroit: Visible Ink Press, 1993.

Clark, Jerome, and Loren Coleman. "Swamp Slobs Invade Illinois." *Fate Magazine*, July 1974.

Coleman, Jerry. *Strange Highways*. Alton, IL: Whitechapel Press, 2003.

———. *More Strange Highways*. Decatur, IL: Whitechapel Press, 2006.

Coleman, Loren. *Bigfoot*. New York: Paraview Pocket Books, 2003.

———. *Curious Encounters*. Winchester, MA: Faber & Faber, 1985.

———. *Mothman & Other Curious Encounters*. New York: Paraview Pocket Books, 2002.

———. *Mysterious America*. Winchester, MA: Faber & Faber, 1983.

———. "Mystery Animals Invade Illinois." *Fate Magazine*, March 1971.

Fliege, Stu. *Tales and Trails of Illinois*. Champaign, IL: University of Illinois Press, 2002.

Guiley, Rosemary Ellen. *Atlas of the Mysterious in North America*. New York: Facts on File, 1995.

Hall, Mark. *Thunderbirds*. New York: Paraview Pocket Books, 2004.

Hunt, Gerry. *Bizarre America*. New York: Berkley, 1988.

Keel, John. *Complete Guide to Mysterious Beings*. New York: Doubleday, 1994.

Monaco, Richard. *Bizarre America 2*. New York: Berkley, 1992.

Pohlen, Jerome. *Oddball Illinois*. Chicago: Chicago Review Press, 2000.

Rath, Jay. *I-Files*. Madison, WI: Trails Media Group, 1999.

Shoemaker, Michael T. "The Mad Gasser of Botetourt." *Fate Magazine,* June 1985.

Taylor, Troy. *Haunted Illinois*. Alton, IL: Whitechapel Press, 2004.

———. *Into the Shadows*. Alton, IL: Whitechapel Press, 2003.

———. *Mysterious Illinois*. Decatur, IL: Whitechapel Press, 2006.

———. *Out Past the Campfire Light*. Alton, IL: Whitechapel Press, 2003.

———. *Weird Illinois*. New York: Sterling Publications, 2005.

Westrum, Ron. "Phantom Attackers." *Fortean Times* 45 (Winter 1985).

NEWSPAPERS

Alton Telegraph
Charleston Daily Courier
Chicago Daily News
Chicago Herald Examiner
Chicago Sun-Times
Chicago Tribune
Decatur Herald & Review
Mattoon Daily Journal-Gazette

ABOUT THE AUTHOR

Troy Taylor is the author of more than eighty books on history, crime, mysteries, and the supernatural in America. He was born and raised in Illinois and currently resides in an undisclosed location in Chicago.

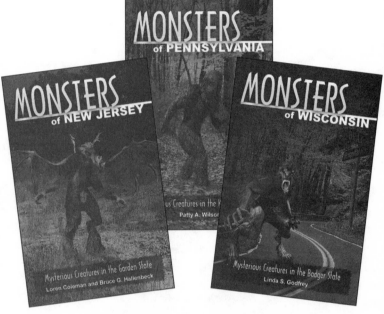